Motorbooks International
POWERPRO SERIES

AUTOMOTIVE TOOLS
HANDBOOK

David H. Jacobs, Jr.

First published in 1993 by Motorbooks International Publishers & Wholesalers, PO Box 2, 729 Prospect Avenue, Osceola, WI 54020 USA

Motorbooks International books are also available at discounts in bulk quantity for industrial or sales-promotional use. For details write to Special Sales Manager at the Publisher's address

Library of Congress Cataloging-in-Publication Data
Jacobs, David H.
    Automotive tools handbook / David H. Jacobs, Jr.
        p.   cm.—(Motorbooks International powerpro series)
    Includes index.
    ISBN 0-87938-712-2
    1. Automobiles—Maintenance and repair—Equipment and supplies.
    I. Title.   II. Series.
    TL152.J293   1993
    629.28'7—dc20   92-29761

On the front cover: A well-equipped shop makes a repair and restoration job go more smoothly. *Jim Poluch, The Eastwood Company*

Printed and bound in the United States of America

Contents

Acknowledgments

Plenty of people have assisted with this book project in a number of different ways. I want to thank all of them for their efforts and enthusiasm.

Dan Mycon, owner of Newlook Autobody in Kirkland, Washington, opened his shop for photography sessions and took time to pose for pictures while using some interesting tools. Art Wentworth lent his tidy garage for photo sessions and participated as a model while pictures were taken of tools. Bill O'Brien made his 1939 Chevrolet four-door sedan available, and Bob Jennings made sure his 1954 Ford F-100 was clean and shiny for pictures. Dan Case helped out with his 1968 Jaguar E Type roadster and 1981 Ferrari 308 GTSi, as well as by posing for a few pictures.

Janna Jacobs was a tremendous help with research, photo organization, and numerous odd jobs. Chuck Stearns, Steve Brown, and Bob Greer pitched in with technical help and hands-on assistance. Van and Kim Nordquist and their crew from Photographic Designs did an outstanding job processing roll after roll of film, taking extra time in the darkroom making sure every print turned out just right.

The staff at Motorbooks International is always eager to help out in any way they can. For their continued support and enthusiasm, I thank Tim Parker, Michael Dregni, Barbara Harold, Greg Field, Michael Dapper, Mary LaBarre, and Cheryl Drivdahl.

Along with extending my sincere gratitude to Jim Poluch and Christine Collins from The Eastwood Company, I thank the following people for providing me with information, photos, and samples of their company's automotive tool or equipment products: Gary Busha, Snap-on; Lauren Cox, Black and Decker; Yvon Desaulniers, Alden Corporation; David Dodd, Sidewinder Products Corporation; Stan Erwine, American Tool Companies; Bob Kindig, Kent-Moore; Al Pacheco, P.C.S.; Gary Devroy, Intermark World Products; David Martel, Harbor Freight Tools; Tammy Peterson, K. O. Lee Company; Michael Brainerd, Dremel; Cindy Sawyers, Porter-Cable; Linda Johnson, Makita U.S.A.; Anne Rottinger, William K. Westley Company; Jeff Noland, HTP America; John Voeller, Neward Enterprises; John Pfanstiehl, Pro Motorcar Products; Jeff Gaul, MSD Ignition; Anita Matthews, Jacobs Electronics; Joel Johnson, Steelcrafters; Allison Zwicker, TiP Sandblast Equipment; Jeff Lock, Foreign Car Specialties; Greg Sivill, Right Angle Tool Company; Joe Christensen, Smithy Company; Bill Cork, Plano Molding Company; Joseph Jolet, Chief Automotive Systems; Colley Matheny, WESCO; Richard Slejza, Lions Automotive; Ken Sakamoto, Sunchaser Tools; Fred LoBianco, California Car Cover Company; Sally Anderson, Chamberlain Group; John Honeycombe, Parking Solutions; Stephen Wilkinson, Bug Brick Products; Josh Malks, Jericho Products; Ann Dennis, O.C.S. Shark File Sharpening System; Tina Sefidvash, SEFIDCo; Empire Brushes; Wayne Thomas, Aeroquip Corporation; John Padden, Sun Belt Products; Donald Burke, Burke Equipment Corporation; Philip Colaiacovo, CooperTools; Timothy Golden, NTY International Corporation; Theodore Cribari, Jr., OMNIVERSE Research; Wayne Maresh, Maresh Industries; Helsper Sewing Company; John Schoepke, Pine Ridge Enterprise; Ron Ballard, Vermont American; Jim De Meo, Eagle Equipment Company; and Bill Miller, Lockdown Securities, Inc.

Preface

When casual mention of automotive tools is made to some general auto enthusiasts, their first thoughts might drift toward wrenches, screwdrivers, socket sets, ratchets, timing lights, and creepers. Talking *tools* to professional autobody technicians will probably start them thinking of body hammers, dollies, flangers, MIG welders, sanders, and other specialty items.

Along with autobody repair specialists, engine mechanics, painters, detailers, customizers, racers, concours competitors, professional restorers, rust-proofers, and serious aficionados rely upon a host of tools and equipment to help their repair and restoration projects flow smoothly and reach completion stages with optimum finish results and minimum hands-on hassles. Some tools are common and are found in the tool chest arsenals of just about everyone who works on cars or trucks. Typically, these would include open-end wrenches, metric- and American-sized sockets, slot- and Phillips-head screwdrivers, pliers of various styles, and an adjustable wrench or two.

Fundamental sets of basic hand tools are generally expected necessities, but as one ponders delving deeper into the internal workings of any machine or part thereof, one must understand that specific tools may be needed to remove or install certain engine, drivetrain, suspension, brake, steering, electrical, and general body parts or assemblies. Combine an absolute requirement for the use of some specialty tools on unique automotive parts with the overall convenience offered by a host of other work-saving tools and equipment options, and you will soon discover that the list of automotive repair instruments, implements, utensils, devices, gadgets, contraptions, mechanisms, and so on is just about never ending.

Since the world of automotive tools and equipment is so vast, it is virtually impossible to include every applicable item inside the covers of just one book. Therefore, this text has been designed as a general guide to introduce a number of companies that manufacture, supply, or distribute all kinds and types of automotive tools and equipment. You should discover a variety of new tools and products that you may not have been exposed to before—but don't stop with just that.

Many of the companies that have participated in this book project also offer a good many other items that could easily save you work or help your auto projects come together much more handily. Take advantage of company address listings to order catalogs and supplemental information about other products. Along with what is featured on the following pages are hundreds of other tools that you may have never dreamed existed; some ultimately may even turn out to be ideal implements for greatly helping you get through particularly intricate or labor-intensive auto repair and restoration operations.

Introduction

Only a few select avid auto enthusiasts are able to get by without owning any tools or auto maintenance equipment items. These are generally wealthy people who have the means to hire professionals who take care of their special automobiles' service and cosmetic needs. Most of us "regular" avid auto enthusiasts, on the other hand, relish our small assortments of hand tools and car care items and cherish opportunities to repair, tinker, tune up, wash, polish, and wax our special rides.

Products like those shown on these pages are available through a number of outlets, such as mail-order and catalog offerings directly from manufacturers, auto parts stores, tool houses, vendors at auto swap meets, retail tool stores, mobile vans from automotive tool companies, and affiliated agencies.

Here are some popular car care tools commonly found in the garages of many avid auto enthusiasts. Along with an array of storage boxes and trays, you should recognize an orbital buffer, floor jack, fender cover, timing light, car duster, and airbrush outfit.

Finding tools and equipment for specific automotive repair or restoration projects may require a trip to a specialty store.

General-purpose tools, like wrenches, sockets, pliers, and screwdrivers, are generally plentiful and easily available through a number of retail outlets. One well-known store is Sears Roebuck and Company, which offers a full range of Craftsman brand hand and power tools. In the Yellow Pages of your telephone book under the heading for tools, you should also be able to locate other tool houses that sell a number of different brands, from cheap imports to high-quality, reliable instruments. Be sure to read warranties, and don't take for granted that all low-cost tools are made just as sturdy as premium models. At times, the savings of just a few dollars on some tools may prove to be a liability when the instruments break the first or second time you use them and you find out that their period of warranty lasts only until you walk out the store's door.

Automotive specialty stores include an autobody paint and supply store, like WESCO Autobody Supply located in Kirkland, Washington. This is a place where you will find tools and equipment geared especially for autobody repair, painting, and detailing. Autobody paint and supply stores are generally frequented by professional autobody and paint specialists, so inventories of tools, equipment, and accessories are most often heavy-duty and of high quality. In addition, since these types of businesses are local outlets for major national and international manufacturers of auto paint, they are kept abreast of most recent technological updates and are usually quick to make newly designed tools and pieces of equipment available, along with up-to-date user instructions and application techniques. Locate autobody paint and supply stores under the Yellow Pages heading for automobile bodyshop equipment and supplies.

If a thorough search through retail tool stores, specialty houses, and other sources found in the Yellow Pages fails to turn up the kinds of tools or equipment you need, try shopping at a local or regional auto swap meet. Many vendors make a living at these events by attending as many as possible throughout various geographical regions. They accumulate inventory resources through contacts made at many custom car shows and other auto events. By communicating with tool and equipment manufacturers, they are frequently able to sell specific products at swap meets not attended by manufacturing companies. Likewise, conversations with lots of auto enthusiasts sometimes lead them to introductions of new products by manufacturing companies in need of additional sales forces.

If you have a keen desire to amass as many tools as possible in the shortest amount of time and with the least amount of money, try used tool stores and pawnshops. Although you will certainly sacrifice the pleasure of owning new tools and any expressed warranty that originally accompanied them, you may be able to get through a few projects, at least until you're able to afford new stuff. In addition, some used tool stores and pawnshops that may feel saddled with unusual tools

Another means of locating tools, especially out-of-the-ordinary ones designed for special applications is through automobile magazines.

they know nothing about could in reality be holding the very special items that you have been looking for all over town.

Another way to locate tools, especially unique ones designed for special applications, is through automobile magazines like *Sport Truck, Custom Rodder, Hemmings Motor News, Car Craft,* and *Hot Rod.* Monthly car magazines are often one of the first places inventors of ingenious auto accessories turn to adver-

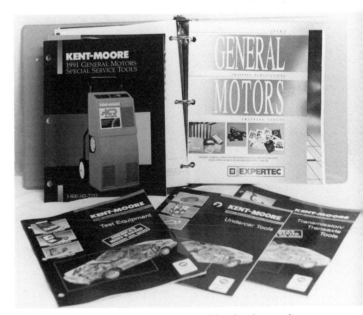

The belief that the special tools required for the dismantling or installation of factory auto assemblies are only available to dealership service departments is largely a misconception. There are many outlets for tools designed for special applications and purposes.

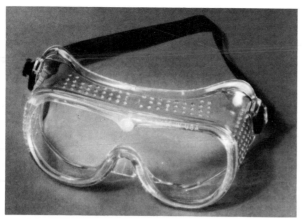

Personal safety is never to be taken lightly. Broken bolts, stripped threads, frayed wires, and punctured hoses can all be replaced; your eyes, ears, and lungs *cannot* be! Whenever using power tools or equipment, hammers, pry bars, or other striking instruments, *always* wear eye protection such as these safety goggles. Just a tiny metal sliver could put out an eye.

tise their new creations. Folks like these frequently have designed particular products out of a genuine need that you could also be faced with. The use of special tools might save you lots of time, money, and

restoration labor or help to better preserve your favorite show car through rough winter weather. Along with special application tools, creative car guys may simply develop better "mousetraps" that will serve intended auto repair or service functions in a more timely and economical manner.

Do-it-yourself mechanics who work on newer cars may often find themselves stymied when attempting to remove auto attributes that were designed to be dismantled with special tool *XYZ*. Once that one-of-a-kind tool is acquired and used, the jobs are generally completed with little or no problem. But where does one find such a tool? Try the parts department at the automobile dealership where your car or truck was purchased, or one that carries the same make and model as your vehicle.

Along with catalogs full of "regular" tools and equipment, Kent-Moore, of SPX Corporation, manufactures and supplies a great many special service tools and related equipment items. Kent-Moore is the special tool supplier for General Motors (GM), Nissan, Hyundai, Isuzu, and other miscellaneous smaller customers. It is also primarily a direct mail-order company that will provide catalogs upon request.

Except among the maverick auto buffs who have been seemingly customizing cars and trucks since their inception, interest in the restoration and repair of

Ideally, a clear face shield such as the one shown here will be worn while a person uses the metal cutoff tool resting next to the shield. Although good goggles can protect your eyes against sparks and slivers, a full face shield offers considerably more overall protection. *The Eastwood Company*

older automobiles was not a widely shared passion until the late 1980s. Tremendous increases in dollar values for antiques and classics have helped to create an atmosphere of eager enthusiasm for older cars from the standpoint of both true auto affection and realistic asset accumulation. Some folks pay handsome sums to have unique machines restored to perfection in order to increase the value of their assets and make money. Others simply appreciate specific makes and models and restore these treasures for the thrill of owning concours winners or vehicles with high intrinsic values.

In the hope of accommodating the enthusiasts who choose to restore automobiles, a number of companies have opened businesses that cater to the tool, equipment, parts, and supply needs of do-it-yourself autobody technicians, mechanics, painters, detailers, and restoration aficionados in general. Many companies advertise their products through monthly car magazines and do-it-yourself home improvement periodicals. Most advertisements carry toll-free telephone numbers or business addresses so potential customers may call or write for catalogs and additional information. Because of increasing costs for catalog printings and mailings, some companies have been forced to charge nominal fees for their catalogs. Prices range from $.50 to $5.00, depending upon catalog size, color content, and other variables.

One could easily liken do-it-yourself auto buffs in tool supply outlets to kids in candy stores. It is entertaining to look at and marvel over ingenious tool inventions—their capabilities and realistic work-saving or finish improvement qualities. Affording everything you would like is one thing, of course, but locating or learning of new or unique items is something else. Look through magazines; order and read catalogs; browse through tool stores; and attend swap meets, car shows, and other auto events to get a realistic perspective of what sort of tools and equipment are available and how much they generally sell for.

If you have a labor-intensive restoration or repair project, especially on an older or foreign automobile, you may do yourself a favor by checking in with a professional restoration shop before actually starting work. Arming yourself with a six-pack of soft drinks and a box of doughnuts may be all it takes to learn of some special tools that will eventually be needed to carefully dismantle or assemble your special vehicle in ways that preserve delicate clips, pins, fasteners, assemblies, components, and so on.

Another source of excellent information with regard to the restoration, modification, or repair of special cars and trucks is local car clubs. Many club members are adamant auto enthusiasts with a keen eye for detail and overall perfection. Their experience and expertise—gained through years of trial-and-error frustration, hand-me-down information from older members of different generations, and hours of re-

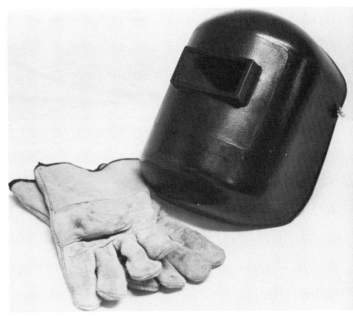

All welding maneuvers require users and bystanders to wear protective helmets equipped with dark lenses. Looking directly at arc welding operations without eye protection can cause eye injuries or total blindness. Dark lenses are available in various shades. The darkest are required for intensely hot welding, while lighter ones may be suitable for low-amperage welding. Charts that are available at welding supply houses designate numerical codes for lenses that are recommended when welding at specific amperage settings and with assorted types of welding materials. Welding helmets are designed so that a clear glass lens can be placed in front of a more expensive dark one, so only the inexpensive clear lens is hit by welding sparks, which are unavoidable. Have a few clear lenses on hand to replace those damaged during long welding operations—they will help you to see a lot better. Wear heavy-duty leather gloves while welding, too. They will save your hands and wrists from becoming pockmarked with tiny burns. *The Eastwood Company*

search in factory shop manuals—could be a bountiful treasure to novice members, not only for locating and acquiring special tools but also for finding out how to achieve rewarding restoration results.

Energetic, talented, and resourceful auto restorers will not let a failure to locate certain special tools stand between them and finishing projects. Confounded by an inability to dismantle a certain assembly because special tools are not available, these aggressive restorers will study tool displays in factory shop manuals and then make their own tools from raw stock using the other tools and equipment at their disposal, occasionally hiring out some intricate work to professional machinists or other craftspeople.

Products are also invented for the express purpose of simply making difficult jobs easier to accomplish. Throughout this book, you should be able to quickly recognize nifty products that were manufactured to make your do-it-yourself restoration endeavors sim-

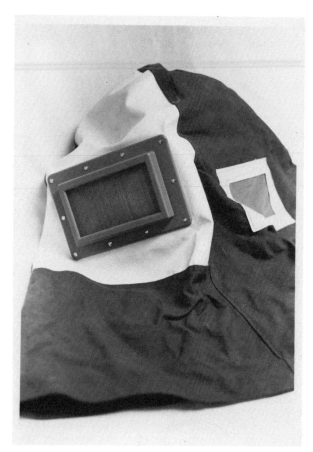

All sandblasting operations require users to wear a full hood and heavy-duty gloves, except operations confined to enclosed sandblasting cabinets. This hood features a large view window with screened ventilation openings on both sides. The hood's inner top section is equipped with a hard hat. Sandblasting operations are noisy procedures, and you should wear some type of ear protection. In addition, especially with specific types of sandblasting media, you must wear a filter mask or respirator. Some types of silica media are irritating to lung tissues and must not be inhaled. Sandblast supply outlets are generally up-to-date on user protection requirements and should be able to advise you adequately about which kind of respiratory protection is best suited for the sandblasting media you plan to use. *The Eastwood Company*

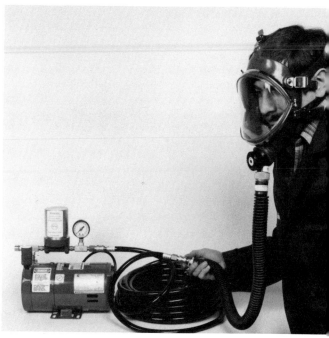

This is one brand of fresh air respirator available to automotive painters. A full face mask is pressurized with fresh air supplied through a dedicated air compressor equipped with appropriate filters. It is the type of respirator that all manufacturers of catalyzed paint products for automobiles strongly recommend painters wear. Paint products that require hardener additives (catalysts) include a form of isocyanate material in their mixtures. Isocyanate products can be extremely harmful to respiratory systems and must not be inhaled. Ordinary particle masks and filter respirators do not adequately filter out isocyanate-impregnated fumes. You are urged to follow manufacturers' recommendations and wear a fresh air respirator every time you paint with any catalyzed product. To be fully protected while painting automobiles, you should also don painter's coveralls, a hood, and latex gloves. These items are commonly available at autobody paint and supply stores. *The Eastwood Company*

pler and much more enjoyable. Short wrenches for tight spots, angled drill motors and special bits, unique ratchets and sockets, and pneumatic and cordless power units are just a few of the kinds of products featured, along with several reliable standbys that have undergone some innovative updating.

Do not allow sanding dust, welding fumes, metal-cutting smoke, and paint overspray to enter your lungs. Use a properly designed filter mask or respirator while engaged in these types of activities. Likewise, save your hearing by wearing ear plugs or protectors while operating loud power tools. Black and Decker offers the safety products featured here. You can also find similar items at safety and supply stores, autobody paint and supply outlets, retail tool houses, and other equipment supply businesses.

A clear face shield is useful while operating grinders, coarse-grit sanding discs, die grinders, bench grinders, and other machines that could throw out sparks, slivers, or metal chips. Consider wearing a lightweight face shield while working under automobile bodies, too. It protects eyes from falling dirt, crud, and debris.

Chapter 1

Mechanic's Hand Tools

Mechanic's hand tools are generally characterized by their ability to be used without power tool attributes. Except for a few that are designed to be operated at the end of a power drill, items featured in this section are all hand operated.

Along with wrenches and screwdrivers, a great many hand tools are available that make working on cars much easier. Ratchets and sockets are wonderful work savers, and some of the newer designs are even more versatile than standard models. Improvements have been made in a number of hand tool categories not only to make auto restoration and repair work easier and faster but also to allow for the rejuvenation of many bolts, threads, and other auto components.

Before using any new tool or piece of equipment, always plan to spend adequate time reading and understanding its operator instructions. Far too often, eager do-it-yourselfers rush to use new tools, only soon and sadly to discover that they have broken the tools or the auto parts the tools were used on. Tools with various settings, alignments, or adjustments must be properly dialed in before any force is applied to them. Incorrectly set, these tools could strip threads, chip gears, or destroy parts. Read directions *before* starting work with new tools to preserve not only the tools and the auto parts you're working on but also the items that surround your work space, as well as your knuckles.

Snap-on Tools Corporation

The product line for Snap-on Tools Corporation includes more than 13,000 items, from sockets and ratchets to sophisticated diagnostic oscilloscopes. Although these products are geared toward the needs of automotive professionals, a great many serious auto enthusiasts also rely on Snap-on quality for their tool needs. Most often, Snap-on tools are available through local sales dealers who provide demonstrations, prices, and on-the-spot service by way of mobile vans. To locate the dealer closest to you, look in the Yellow Pages under the heading for tools.

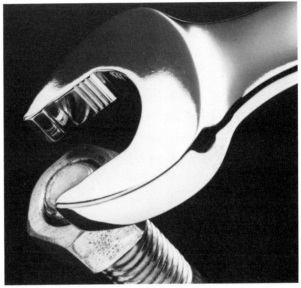

Snap-on says, "Like a bull dog clamped on a table leg, FLANK DRIVE PLUS grabs the sides of a fastener and won't let go." The serrations on the open end of this wrench were strategically placed to increase the tool's torque capability by a full 40 percent. Originally designed for aircraft applications in the 1960s to improve turning power by 15 to 20 percent, this feature was improved dramatically by Snap-on. Serrations help keep nuts seated in wrenches and away from the weaker corners of the fasteners. This feature goes a long way toward reducing the possibility of rounding off fastener heads, along with adding a great deal of turning power. Because FLANK DRIVE PLUS Snap-on Wrenches increase mechanics' ability to put pressure on fasteners, Snap-on notes that the serrations could cause bite marks or blemishes during high-pressure applications. Therefore, standard wrenches are recommended for chrome or decorative nuts and bolts. In American sizes, these serrated wrenches are offered from ³/₈ inch (in) to a full 1in. Overall lengths go from 6¹/₂in for the ³/₈in wrench to a full 14in for the 1in model. Metric sizes are also available, in all sizes from 10 millimeters (mm) to 19mm. Both the open and boxed ends of these wrenches are set at a 15-degree angle to their handle. This provides fast nut turning in restricted areas and also plenty of knuckle clearance over obstructions. Handles are made from a strong carbon alloy steel that is nickel-and-chrome–plated to protect against corrosion and to add a bright finish. They are rounded off to provide a comfortable grip and aid in leverage.

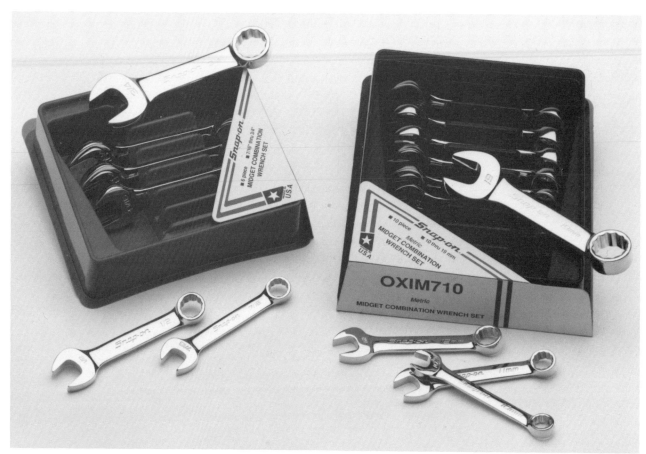

Have you ever wished you had a wrench that was short enough to fit into an extratight space? Even gone so far as to hack off the end of an old one just to finish a project? Well, Snap-on has a solution with its Midget Combination Wrench Sets in both American and metric sizes. The crowded engine compartments of today's new cars would attest to the usefulness of these midget sets. A 15-degree offset on the open end and a 7.5-degree offset on the boxed end allows users to flip wrenches over to acquire new grips. Midget wrenches are made with the same materials and finish as their larger counterparts and span the ranges of 10mm to 19mm for the metric set and $7/16$in to $3/4$in for American sizes.

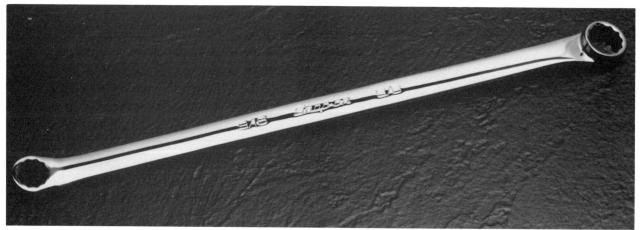

Although you might think that all box-end wrenches are alike, these from Snap-on stand out as preferred tools by aerospace industries. They are designed for use on the high-tensile nuts, bolts, and cap screws commonly found in the aerospace field. This XDH Series of wrenches consists of high-performance tools that feature the Flank Drive wrenching system along with twelve-point boxes for strength and durability. To achieve maximum strength with even dispersal of torquing stress, these tools are precision-machined to provide dimensional control for uniform wall thickness and diameter on the box end. You can get them in a nickel-and-chrome—polished finish or a black industrial finish, ranging in size from $7/32$in to $13/16$in.

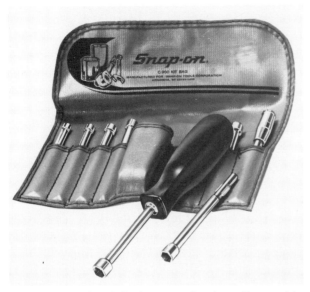

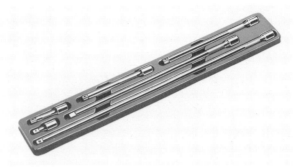

Nut Drivers are handy for the removal and installation of the small nuts scattered throughout most vehicles. They are less cumbersome than ratchets and sockets and can accomplish jobs much faster than wrenches in many cases where strong leverage is not needed. As opposed to providing sets with a single shaft and a series of individual sockets, Snap-on offers this kit with sockets solidly attached to 4in blades. This enables users to grip blades while pulling sockets loose from sticky nuts instead of having to reach into tight spaces with their fingers alone to remove sockets stuck in place on top of fasteners. The kit includes a 4in extension blade along with a screwdriver handle and convenient carrying case. Sizes range from $3/16$in to $3/8$in.

Anyone who works on automobiles knows the value of socket and ratchet sets and the benefits of having a few extensions on hand. Snap-on's Extension Set has an added feature: knurled grip sections. Starting a nut or bolt deep inside an engine or body cavity is not always easy to do, especially when fingers cannot reach inside the immediate area. Starting fasteners with a ratchet is dangerous, as it is easy to cross-thread them. Frequently, mechanics and technicians start fasteners using a ratchet extension attached to a socket. This allows them to *feel* nuts or bolts starting and avoid cross-threading. Many times, however, obtaining a firm grip on extensions is made difficult by hand oils, perspiration, and engine grease. This is where the knurling feature on these extensions comes in handy. It provides fingers with a filelike texture, enabling users to firmly grasp the extensions for steady maneuvering and the chance to feel fasteners attach correctly. The extension set shown here includes units in lengths of $1^1/4$in, 2in, 4in, 6in, 10in, and 14in.

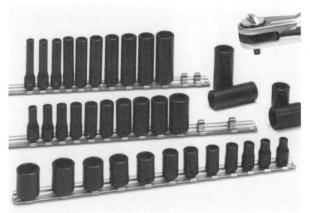

Snap-on's $1/4$in Square Drive Sealed Ratchets are lubricated with an oil-graphite substance and sealed in such a way that internal friction is reduced and debris is kept out. This eliminates the need to tear down, clean, and lubricate ratchets to keep them in clog-free and maneuverable working condition. Three seals are designed into the head of these ratchets: a gear seal, pawl seal, and cover plate O-ring. Snap-on recommends that its sealed ratchets be cleaned with a light-grade oil in lieu of paint thinners or solvents. Here, the long ratchet at the top has a length of $6^1/2$in, the shorter model in the center is $4^7/16$in long, and the Flex-Head unit at the bottom has a 6in shaft length. Each features a thirty-tooth gear unit with action set at 12 degrees.

More and more, auto enthusiasts are turning toward pneumatic ratchets to help their restoration and repair projects progress at a more rapid pace. The problem is, not every socket set is designed for use with air-driven impact wrenches; most are simply not designed or built strong enough to withstand some of the heavy pressures impact wrenches apply to them. This set is different. It has been developed for use with Snap-on's FAR25 $1/4$in Drive Air Ratchet, which operates at 90 pounds per square inch gauge (psig). The sockets are heat-treated especially for impact applications, and all twelve units range in size from 5mm to 15mm, including a 5.5mm socket. The lower set is a standard length, the middle is semideep, and the top is deep. The drive ends are marked with knurling for easy identification. Socket rails come with the package, but the $1/4$in Square Drive Air Ratchet is sold separately.

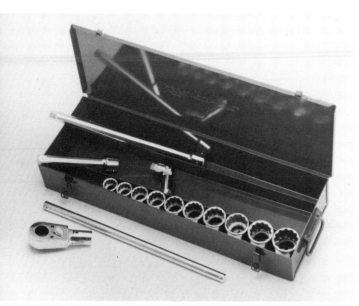

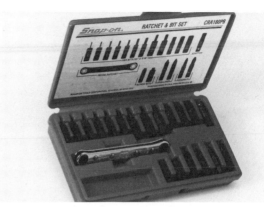

The Snap-on heavy-duty 15-Piece ³/₄in Drive Socket Set has ten sockets that are all twelve-point models and range in size from 1¹/₆in to 1⁷/₈in. Also included are a ratchet head, a 20in handle, a breaker bar, and 8in and 16in extensions. The metal carrying case is optional. A heavy-duty socket set over and beyond standard ¹/₂in drives is not normally required for use on standard cars or trucks. In fact, this outfit was initially designed for service on tractors, buses, other heavy-duty vehicles, and industrial machinery. Off-road enthusiasts, big-time 4x4 enthusiasts, and those with heavyweight machinery, however, may be impressed with the versatility of this industrial-sized socket set built to withstand the rigors of maximum torque and tightening needs.

When hex-head fasteners are tightly torqued into position, one wonders if simple hex keys are strong enough to remove them. With the Snap-on Ratchet and Bit Set, those worries are over. The slim-line design allows access into tight areas, and plenty of torque is possible by using the ratchet in a levered position, just like a wrench. Each bit is equipped with a rubber retaining ring that secures it into the ratchet with just slight hand pressure; you don't have to use your free hand to keep bits in place while setting them into fasteners. The set features bits in hex, square, Phillips, and POZIDRIV configurations in a variety of sizes from ¹/₂₀in to ¹/₄in, including #1 and #2 Phillips and #1 and #2 POZIDRIV sizes.

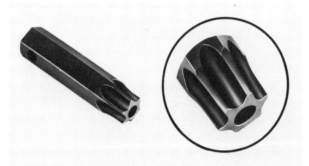

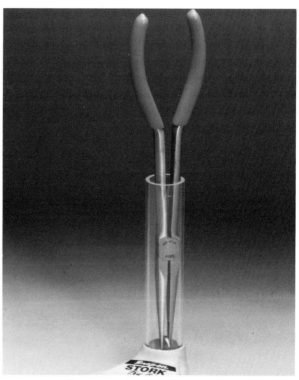

To the untrained eye, all TORX Bits may look alike. In fact, you may not initially notice anything unique about this Snap-on TORX Bit illustration. For those in the know, however, this TORX Bit is special. A hole in the center is the key. Tamperproof TORX fasteners are equipped with a peg in the center to prohibit the use of ordinary TORX Bits for their removal. These special fasteners may adorn newer car assemblies for any of a variety of reasons and could confuse novice do-it-yourself repair persons trying to remove damaged parts and replace them with new ones. These bits will work with a ¹/₄in bit-type screwdriver, ¹/₄in or ⁵/₁₆in bit-holding ratchet, or other square-drive tool in conjunction with an appropriate socket. The set carries ten TORX sizes ranging from T8 to T50.

Snap-on's Stork is a superlong needle-nose pliers. Its unique design allows the retrieval of items in spaces as narrow as ³/₄in and as deep as 6in, as illustrated here. The overall length of this tool is 11in, and the jaws alone measure 3¹/₄in long. The outside dimension of the tool's head and neck is a mere ¹¹/₁₆in. Another excellent feature of this tool is the precision-aligned jaws. They are designed so that the jaw tips make initial contact, thus maximizing gripping power.

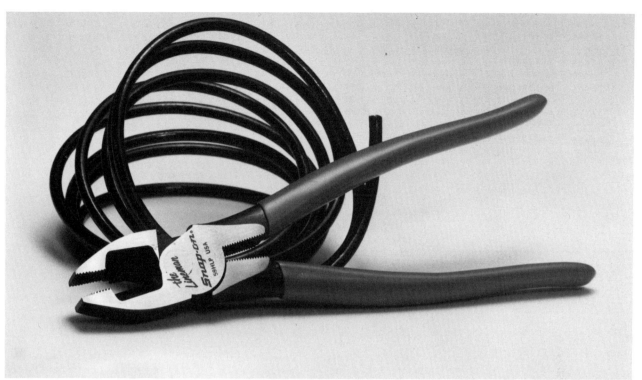

The Heavy-duty Lineman's Pliers can come in handy for a variety of automotive needs. Although basically designed for electrical wiring work on houses and buildings, this tool can easily cut battery cables stretched from an engine compartment back to the trunk space for the pro-street machines and race cars that feature trunk-mounted battery trays. Gripping power is increased when the jaw teeth located on the handle side of the swivel head are used. Snap-on employs a special "draw" broaching process to cut jaw teeth, and then heat-treats each tool for increased strength and durability. Much more than just a wire- or cable-cutting tool, the Heavy-duty Lineman's Pliers may be just the thing you need to hold rusty and rounded-off fasteners secure on one end while loosening them or cutting off their opposite end.

Automobiles built a few decades ago had steering wheels that could be removed with just a simple, universal puller. Newer cars with ignition switches on the steering columns make pulling steering wheels a bit more complex. Lock plates are designed into these units to freeze the steering wheels in one position when the ignition is switched off. This design is intended to be an antitheft measure. To remove these locking units, special pullers are required that depress locking plates so that surrounding fasteners can be loosened. Snap-on's CJ131P Steering Wheel and Lock Plate Depressor Set includes a yoke and selection of bolts for servicing all major American automobiles, along with metric- and American-sized adapters for servicing lock plates. This set is also compatible with the tilt steering wheel models featured on American Motors (AMC), Chrysler, Ford, and GM automobiles.

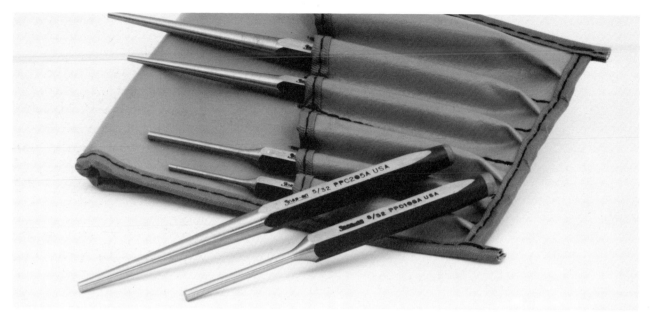

Novice do-it-yourselfers have used everything from 16d nails to bolts as punches for removing pins from all sorts of car parts. As one would expect, these makeshift items generally do not work very well. The only way to remove pins safely and effectively, while preserving pin finishes, is to use a proper-sized punch. Since punches are designed to be smacked with a mallet or hammer, Snap-on uses a process called differential heat treat, which reduces hardness and increases toughness, to draw down the end hit by a hammer. The anvil end, or head, is machined to a modified parabolic curve that directs striking forces toward the center of the head. Thus, when the head is struck, the metal tends to mushroom, with less chance of splitting or cracking. Users are encouraged to periodically dress the striking end of these punches to increase tool longevity. This kit includes punch point edge sizes of 1/8in, 5/32in, 3/16in, 7/32in, 1/4in, and 5/16in. Punch lengths range from 7 1/4in to 8 3/4in. The handling shafts of these punches are designed in a hex fashion to provide a solid grip and good holding strength.

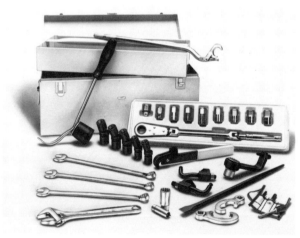

Bushings must be installed correctly. If they are not, they may fail and cause damage to related parts. Bushing driver adapters that are just a fraction of an inch off in size are sometimes all it takes to ruin or damage new bushings. As more vehicles are delivered with combinations of American- and metric-sized parts, consider the inclusion of the Snap-on Metric Bushing Driver Set in your tool arsenal. It offers ten *dual-sized* adapters that will fit twenty of the most common metric bushings. Two drivers are included. An 8in driver is suitable for all ten adapters, and a lighter-duty 7in driver can be used for the five smallest adapters. A 1/2in-20 nut is used to hold adapters on drivers. It has a knurled outer edge for increased gripping strength.

Tools used for wheel alignment are not always universally adaptable to all makes and models of American cars and trucks and import vehicles. To accommodate those who align wheels on a variety of vehicles, Snap-on offers its WA2500WA Wheel Alignment Service Set, which includes the most-requested alignment tools. (Toolbox is optional.) Along with a 20in pry bar and a 12in adjustable wrench, this set includes individual swivel impact sockets in metric sizes for the caster-camber adjustments on Chrysler and GM vehicles, a Ford caster-camber hook set, a four-wheel-drive spanner socket, and sets of additional swivel impact sockets and wrenches. A tie rod tool for cars is provided, as are tie rod tools for trucks and front-wheel-drive vehicles. The carbide burr set, bottom right, is used to elongate alignment adjustment slots.

Vermont American Tool Company

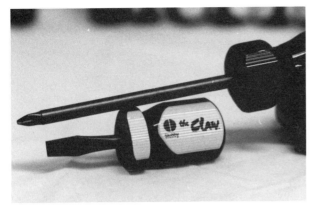

Screwdrivers have been around for over 300 years. Both slot and Phillips tools are seen as simple and practical tools that serve many purposes without any real need for design improvement. Well, Vermont American has engineered a new screwdriver design called The Claw which delivers more screwdriving power, torque, and control with less effort and greater user comfort. Blades on both slot and Phillips screwdriver tips are equipped with Anti-Camout Ribs (ACR) that grip fastener heads tightly to reduce slippage and camout, reducing the potential for damage to screw heads and work surfaces. A user gains more driving power and torque because of the ribbed tips, especially since they're combined with a new ergonomically designed triangular tool handle. The shape of these handles closely resembles the contour of a user's hand when holding tools, resulting in more twisting power with less effort and greater comfort. Each screwdriver is color coated for quick identification: yellow for slotted and red for Phillips. To last long and hold up under rugged use, each tool is manufactured through an exclusive Iso-Temp Process that provides extra tough, fracture resistant bars and tips.

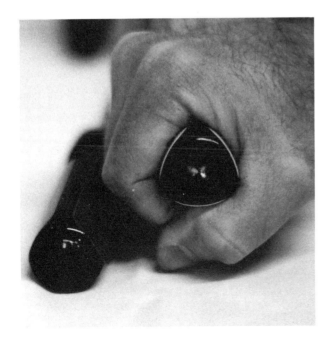

Black and Decker

Black and Decker manufactures and distributes a wide variety of tool and equipment products, from sanders, buffers, die grinders, and air files under its Viking product line, to a host of other products ranging from wet-dry vacuums and drill bits to HeliCoil Thread Repair Kits and power buffers. Products are carried by a number of retail outlets. Use the company's toll-free telephone number to locate a nearby sales outlet or request catalog information.

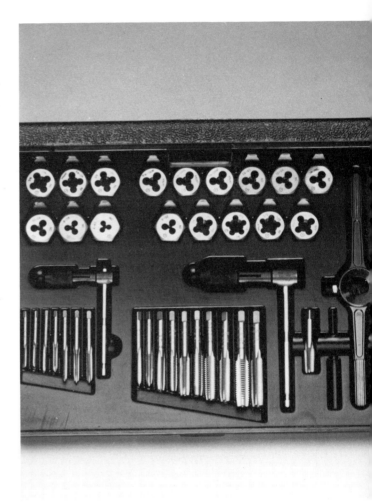

Any do-it-yourself auto enthusiast who says he or she has never stripped a thread is either exceptionally lucky or pulling your leg. Occasionally, bolt or screw holes get stripped or used fasteners need thread rejuvenation. In lieu of sending this type of work out to professionals, you have the option of repairing the damage yourself with the help of the 38-Piece Fractional Tap and Die Set from Black and Decker. In addition, you can even make new or special fasteners— like U-bolts, threaded tension rods, and custom attributes for modified vehicles—with this set using stock materials. Black and Decker also offers a metric tap and die set identical to the one shown here. Read the application instructions before putting this set to use, and adhere to recommendations regarding lubrication requirements.

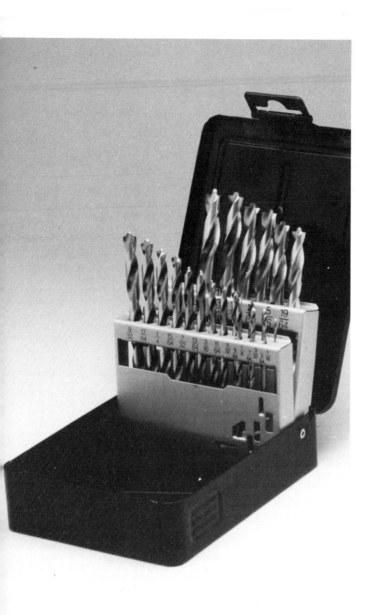

All drill bits are *not* created equal. Normal drill bits tend to walk on metal, to mar surfaces, unless center punch guides are made. They may also lock up at breakthrough, produce burrs, or drill oblong holes. The 21-Piece Bullet Pilot Point HSS Drill Bit Set from Black and Decker is designed to alleviate those kinds of drilling problems. The exclusive Pilot Point design, recognized as a small tip on the business end of drill bit bodies, eliminates walking; keeps bits on course for fast, accurate drilling; and reduces the chances of lockup once bits break through drilled material. In addition, these innovative drill bits feature enlarged flute chambers to maximize chip removal and prevent binding when drilling deep holes. Acute cutting edges located just behind the Pilot Point increase drilling speed and produce a clean, smooth hole with minimal burrs. A back-taper design on the flutes minimizes friction for less wear and longer life. A longer life for drill bits is also enhanced if users apply proper lubrication when drilling in metal materials. Black and Decker's Pilot Point drill bits can be sharpened using dressed grinding wheels; be sure to follow sharpening instructions carefully.

Black and Decker's Screw Extractor Set is useful for both wood and metal applications when screw heads are damaged and no longer removable by conventional means or when heads have completely broken off, leaving behind just a screw shaft. Before extractors are applied, a hole must be carefully drilled into broken screw shafts. Start with a small drill bit to get an accurate guide hole in position. Enlarge that hole with a bigger drill bit to accommodate a properly sized extractor. Screw extractors are designed with reversed threads; twist them in a counterclockwise rotation to tighten them into the holes drilled in broken screws. As the extractors grip more solidly and become imbedded deeper inside the holes, the broken screws are loosened and twisted out of their position. Refrain from providing just small, shallow holes for extractors, as these will allow only the tip of the tool to penetrate broken screw shafts and thus increase the possibility of breaking off the tip. Instead, drill deep, wide holes so that the strongest sections of the extractor body are better equipped to handle the torque needed to remove the fasteners.

Alden Corporation

The Alden Corporation spent over eighteen months testing and researching its DRILL-OUT Broken Bolt Extractor until it was fully satisfied that this product was ready for market. Customer satisfaction was a primary consideration, and it was not until the DRILL-OUT proved itself over and over again that the company finally made way for the tool's distribution.

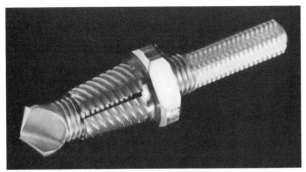

The Alden Corporation has come up with an innovative way to remove broken bolts with DRILL-OUT Broken Bolt Extractor units. These tools combine a sure-fire drilling tip with a collet that makes the extraction of broken bolts a snap. Kits contain four extractors like the one shown here. They can accommodate both American and metric sizes: 1/4in and 6mm, 5/16in and 8 mm, 3/8in and 10mm, and 1/2in and 12mm. Broken Bolt Extractors are reusable, and their tips are self-centering. A self-centering point on drill units enables users to overcome problems associated with finding the center of broken bolts, even when breaks are jagged. A reversible drill motor is required, as extractors are designed to be drilled and twisted into broken bolts in a counterclockwise rotation. The DRILL-OUT is designed to efficiently extract broken bolts in one quick, reliable operation. Alden Corporation offers an instructional videotape that shows exactly how these tools are designed to be used; you are encouraged to order one along with the kit. Note: Wear eye protection any time you work with power tools, especially when cutting or drilling metal.

Alden Corporation DRILL-OUT Broken Bolt Extractors work very well for bolts that have broken flush with or below surfaces. They also do a good job of extracting rusty bolts. You may have trouble removing bolts broken off inside exhaust manifolds, as these fasteners have sometimes been *welded* into position through lots of exposure to extreme heat. Using the Broken Bolt Extractors is easy. After choosing the correct-sized extractor, insert it into a reversible drill adjusted to operate in the reverse mode. Twist the collet up to the drill chuck. Center punch the broken bolt to guarantee a perfect start. For bolts broken off inside of flanges, reverse the collet on the drill body, twist it down next to the drilling tip, and use the collet's flat side as a centering guide. Once a hole has been drilled 1/2in deep, stop the drill motor and position the collet so its threads are stationed just two to four drill bit threads away from the drilling tip (see previous illustration). Then, place the tool back into the newly drilled hole; bring the drill motor up to full speed, still in the reverse mode; and plunge the unit into the hole. The collet will engage with the broken bolt and twist it out. If your drill motor stalls at this point, use a wrench to twist the collet in a counterclockwise direction for bolt removal. Remember: Wear eye protection during this operation, and use a lubricating oil while drilling to preserve the unit's cutting edge.

The Eastwood Company

The Eastwood Company is much more than just a source for automotive repair and restoration tools, equipment, and supplies. It is specifically geared toward a customer base of do-it-yourself auto restorers and those who prefer to complete their own auto maintenance tasks. Along with over 100 pages of catalog items, the company offers customers a free telephone number for technical support. That's right; you can call Eastwood toll free, Monday through Friday, between 8:00 a.m. and 9:00 p.m. Eastern time for technical advice about your restoration project and use of Eastwood's products.

Internal rethread cutters are shaped somewhat like bolts and are designed to rejuvenate the threads on nuts. Conversely, external cutting units look like nuts and are designed to restore threads on bolts. Lubricating oil helps to make cutting easier along with preserving cutting edges. As you discover bad spots on fasteners, slowly work rethreaders back and forth in lieu of forcing them on in a single motion. In addition, always be certain the rethreaders you have selected are the correct size and thread configuration. NC rethreaders (silver in color and shown here in front of a wrench and kit) will not work on SAE-NF threads. If you are confused as to which rethreader to use, try operating one on a nut or bolt in good condition that is identical to the one you want to restore. Rethreaders will easily twist onto same-sized nuts and bolts.

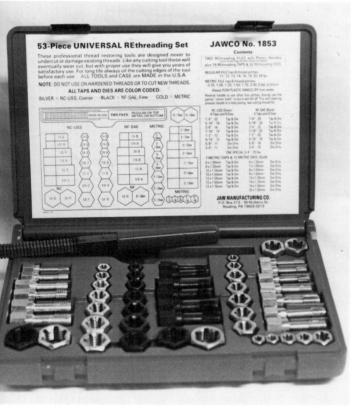

Those who restore older automobiles may sometimes be unable to find factory original nuts, bolts, and other fasteners that perfectly match others used in the design of their special automobile. Except in cases where fasteners are totally destroyed, the 53-Piece Universal Rethreading Set from The Eastwood Company may be ideally suited for the rejuvenation of worn, nicked, or marred threads on nuts, bolts, screws, and other threaded attributes. This is *not* a tap and die set, and users are advised *not* to use these tools for cutting new threads on raw stock. Rather, use them to restore existing threads to like-new condition. Internal and external cutters in this kit are color-coded according to thread specifications: National Coarse (NC), silver; Society of Automotive Engineers National Fine (SAE-NF), black; and metric, gold. Two thread files are also included to dress both SEA and metric threads. To keep cutters in optimum condition, apply lubricating oil during use.

In lieu of a complete rethreading kit, The Eastwood Company also offers small sets of Rethreading Dies. As with the 53-Piece Universal Rethreading Set, these dies are designed to clean and straighten existing threads, not cut new ones. Kits like these are available in a variety of sizes. They range from 1/4in to 1 1/4in and conform to both NC-USS (coarse-thread) and SAE-NF (fine-thread) specifications.

The Universal Thread Cutter from Eastwood is very versatile. It works on all thread sizes, coarse or fine, up to 3/4in. The cutting blades move slightly from side to side to accommodate the threaded item clamped in its jaws. You can use this tool on bolts, studs, and other threaded items that may be permanently affixed to auto attributes. The tool can maneuver in tight spaces on items that cannot be removed but need threads cleaned or straightened. You can repair threads on engine parts, frame and suspension assemblies, and even body sections, Detailed instructions accompany this tool; follow them closely. An arrow on the face of the thread cutter indicates the correct rotation direction.

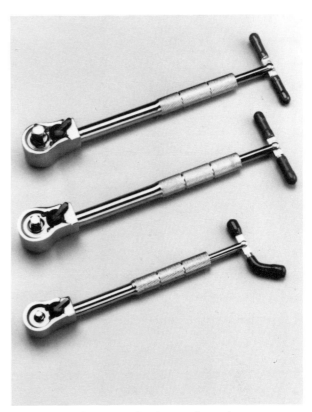

Operating ratchets in confined spaces is not always as easy as one would hope. To be sure, a slow tedious job of moving a ratchet back and forth just one or two clicks at a time can be nerve-racking. At last, a tool is available that operates as a ratchet but also offers a unique accessory feature that allows users to hold the handle steady and simply twist a lever to loosen nuts and bolts. Conventional ratchets and wrenches require plenty of operating room for maneuvering. The Sidewinder Speedwrenches don't. One 360-degree revolution of the handle lever is equal to at least eight standard ratchet revolutions. These tools come in 1/4in, 3/8in, and 1/2in drives. The 1/2in model has been tested to withstand 190 pounds-feet (lb-ft) of torque. All models carry a lifetime warranty. More information about Sidewinder Speedwrenches is also available through Sidewinder Products Corporation, 320 Second Avenue North, Birmingham, AL 35204.

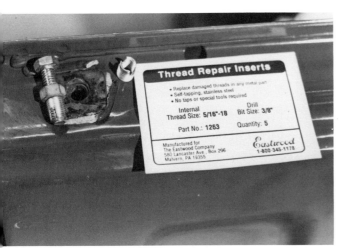

Inevitably, auto restorers and repair persons are faced with damaged threads that cannot be simply rethreaded or easily repaired to usable condition. This tailgate hinge-bolt unit is just such a problem. Eastwood offers Seal-Lock Thread Repair Inserts that are a snap to install and do a great job of securing bolts and screws that are subsequently torqued into them. According to the directions, damaged thread openings are drilled out to a diameter commensurate with an insert's size. Along with an insert, you'll need a bolt or screw that fits inside the damaged opening, as well as inside the insert, and a nut that fits the bolt or screw. The bolt or screw, nut, and insert are used together for the installation, and you will need hand tools both to twist the nut and to secure the bolt or screw. Inserts come in four sizes: 1/4-20, 5/16-18, 3/8-16, and 7/16-14. They can be used in many different situations, including cast-iron or aluminum heads and blocks.

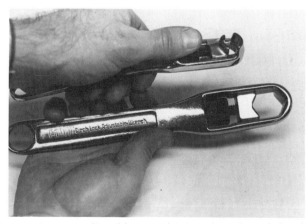

To install a new Seal-Lock Thread Insert: After an appropriate-sized drill bit is used to ream out the damaged thread area, place a compatible nut onto the designated bolt. Then screw on an insert with its slotted end at the bottom; it will be the part that twists into the drilled hole first. Be sure the insert is fully engaged onto the bolt. Run the nut down until it makes contact with the top of the insert. Then, start the unit into the drilled hole and twist it in as far as you can by hand. Use a socket and ratchet or a wrench to hold the bolt in place. Use another wrench to rotate the nut in a clockwise direction. This will cause the thread insert to rotate along with the nut and be screwed into the hole. Continue until the nut meets flush with the surrounding surface. The insert should be fully in place. While still holding the bolt secure, unscrew the nut in a counterclockwise direction. Once the nut has released its grip on the insert, the bolt can be removed. Take the nut off and use the bolt as needed inside the new insert.

Sometimes, an adjustable wrench is just about the only hand tool that will accomplish specific jobs. The Pocket Socket adjustable box wrenches from Eastwood grab four sides of a nut or bolt to make a secure connection. Along with providing a tight grip, the design allows for use in confined areas, like around a hold-down bolt on this air compressor motor. A six-sided head arrangement allows these wrenches to surround fasteners and distribute torque evenly. In addition, protruding factions at the base of the head lets users slip the wrenches over nuts or bolts that are imbedded into designed wells and other shallow openings. The wrenches are available in two sizes: one for fasteners from $5/16$in to $3/4$in and another that fits nuts and bolts from $3/8$in to $1^1/8$in. They also fit metric sizes.

Removing vacuum switches and oil pressure sending units is easy with the help of these special sockets. Vacuum switches feature protruding arms that make it impossible for regular deep sockets to work. Likewise, oil pressure sending units are shaped in such a way that ordinary sockets cannot fit correctly around them. Eastwood's Vacuum Switch Socket is a 7/8in size that has a section cut out of its side through which switch protrusions can extend. This socket will fit over most Ford, GM, and Chrysler vacuum switches. The Oil Pressure Switch Socket, right, is outfitted with a series of multiple indentations that correspond to the exact shape of most oil pressure sending units. It is essentially a 1 1/16in socket that has been designed to accommodate oil pressure switches. Both sockets are operated with a 3/8in-drive ratchet.

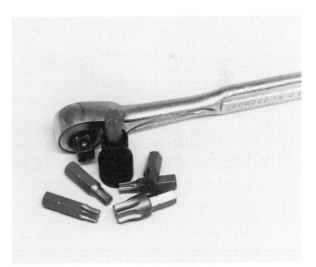

The Eastwood Company's TORX Bit Set includes six bits that are designed to service Ford, GM, Chrysler, and AMC products. An adapter makes it possible to use these bits in conjunction with a 3/8in-drive ratchet. Sizes include the T-30, T-40, T-45, T-50, and T-55 and a special 6mm spline-drive bit. Bits are heat-treated for strength and are essential for the removal or tightening of ordinary TORX fasteners. Never try to get by with a Phillips-head screwdriver when working with TORX fasteners. You may be able to loosen further fasteners that are already loose, but you will surely round out and ruin those which are securely torqued.

Dan Case has owned his 1981 Ferrari 308 GTSi for quite some time. An avid auto enthusiast and perfectionist, he is frequently detailing and servicing his black beauty. One of his common frustrations has been the limited access for reaching the spark plugs at the front of his Ferrari's rear-mounted engine. Introduction to the Sidewinder Speed-wrench lit up Case's eyes, as he immediately recognized this tool's potential value in removing and replacing those hard-to-reach spark plugs and other awkwardly located items. As with any ratchet and socket or wrench, always try to get spark plugs, bolts, and nuts started straight by hand before cinching them down with a tool. This small consideration will go a long way toward eliminating the possibility of stripping or cross-threading fasteners.

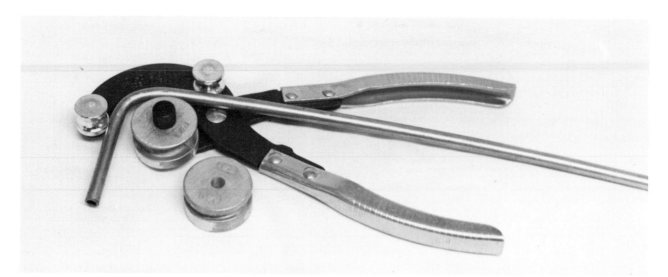

Automobile restorers and those who build custom machines are almost always in need of a tool designed to bend tubing material. New tubing is generally required for modified engine compartments and suspension assemblies when brake, fuel, or vacuum lines have to be rerouted. Eastwood's Tubing Bender makes this type of work easy. The tool is equipped to handle copper and steel tubing in ³/₁₆in, ¹/₄in,

⁵/₁₆in, and ³/₈in sizes. Roller adapters that come with the tool make tight bends without collapsing tube walls. Rollers are clearly marked to help you determine which one is designed for specific tubing dimensions. Used incorrectly, the wrong-sized rollers might tend to flatten tube walls instead of providing smooth curves.

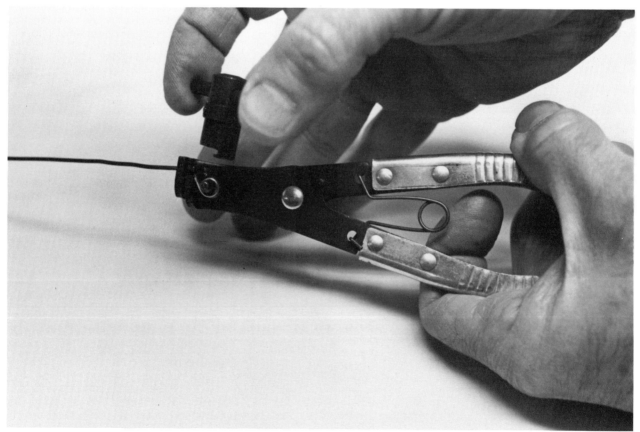

Heater units, vents, and other automobile accessories are frequently operated by means of heavy-duty single-wire cables. Cable ends are coiled and then slipped over pins on activating mechanisms. One easy way to coil the ends of

cables is with a special tool, like the Cable Coiling Pliers from Eastwood. The tip design of this tool is engineered to hold a cable in one position while an accessory is used to twist the cable end around a pin. The operation is simple and quick.

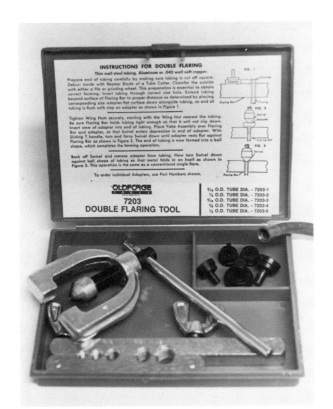

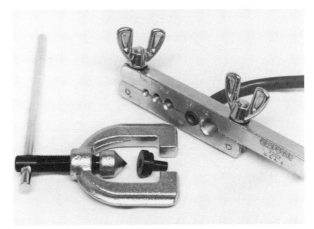

To produce a double flare using the Eastwood Double-Single Flaring Tool, first determine the size tubing in use and select the appropriate-sized adapter. First photo: Insert the tube into the yoke and let it extend out past the yoke surface a distance equal to the adapter's indicative marking lip. Second photo: Next, insert the adapter's pin end into the tube and position the tapered ram swivel over it. Use the hand lever to screw down the ram swivel, forcing the adapter to bend the tube end. Once the adapter is flush with the yoke, back off the ram swivel and remove the adapter. Third photo: Then, simply force the ram swivel into the tube end to complete the second stage of the double flare.

Tubing lines must be flared at their ends to ensure proper sealing of their couplings. The Double-Single Flaring Kit from Eastwood allows you to complete double compression flares for brake lines or single compression flares for fuel lines and other lines on steel, aluminum, and copper tubing. It is *not* recommended for stainless steel tubing or materials over $1/25$in thick. Adapters can accommodate $3/16$in, $1/4$in, $5/16$in, $3/8$in, and $1/2$in tubing. Instructions are concise and are found on the kit's cover. In the top right corner of the kit, next to the adapters, you will notice a completed double flare on a copper tube end.

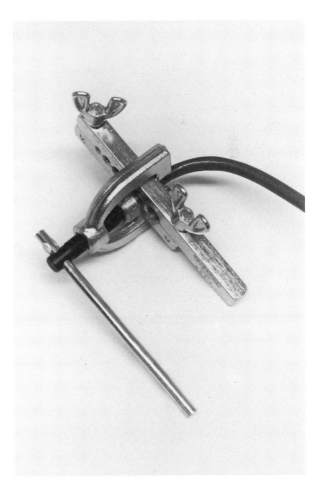

To many serious do-it-yourself aficionados, rebuilding engines involves much more than just the replacement of old parts and installation of new gaskets and seals. These people prefer to go a few steps further, some even more than others. Basically, though, the Block Prep Kit is ideal for smoothing the inside of rough engine castings to speed oil drain-back to the pan and oil pump. Abrasive rolls are twisted onto a mandrel, which is then secured to a drill or die grinder. These handy items remove bits and sharp edges from iron that could otherwise eventually break off to clog a pump or damage other engine parts. Abrasive rolls are available in two shapes: cylindrical and tapered. Three grit textures are also offered: fine (320), medium (240), and coarse (120). You can use these items not only for engine work but for many other restoration chores.

Holding alternators, air conditioning compressors, and power steering units in place while attempting to tighten or adjust belts is not always easy. At times, one may wish one had three or four arms. To help simplify these operations, Eastwood carries the Fan Belt Tightener, which adjusts to put and hold tension on alternators, generators, and the like while you tighten their affected bolts and nuts. The unit comes in four sections and can expand from just 5in to a full 13½in. A hex shaft, left, is rotated to increase or decrease tension. When using this tool, be certain it rests against sturdy support and not just handy protrusions, as a great deal of pressure could be applied to it. In addition, consider draping a heavy cloth or small section of rugged cardboard between tool ends and their resting spots to prevent accidental scratching or surface marring.

Getting old gasket material and sealant off of engine surfaces can be a painstaking chore, especially when attempting to avoid gouging the surface with a putty knife or other scraper. Scotchbrite Cookies were designed for the express purpose of removing stubborn baked-on gasket residue from engine decks, head surfaces, oil pan rails, and anywhere else. Eastwood's Gasket Cleaning Kit includes ten cleaning discs equipped with a Velcro backing that attaches to a standard mandrel. Slower speeds are most suitable for these items, and it is recommended they be used with electric drills as opposed to fast-spinning die grinders or other high-speed units.

American Tool Companies

American Tool Companies manufactures and distributes familiar tool and equipment name brands such as VISE-GRIP, QUICK-GRIP, PROSNIP, UNIBIT, and CHESCO. Its products are sold through many outlets, both retail and mail order. Chances are, the tool supply dealer you frequent the most carries one or more of the firm's brands. If not, contact American Tool Companies to locate a nearby tool or equipment source that handles its products.

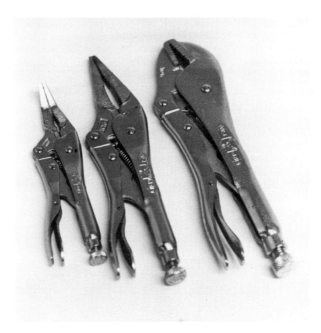

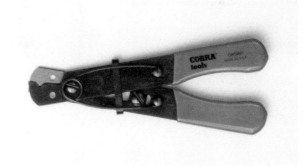

VISE-GRIP Locking Pliers are popular throughout the automotive world. Their jaws can be adjusted to clamp down on objects almost as solidly as a bench vise would. A knurled screw on one handle adjusts gripping tension, and a lever on the opposite handle releases pressure when tasks have been completed. To complement VISE-GRIP regular-nose pliers, American Tool Companies has developed other pliers with special features, like the bent-nose and long-nose models shown here. A number of other useful products are made available by American Tool Companies, like the COBRA-brand V Stripper, also pictured here.

VISE-GRIP bent-nose locking pliers and long-nose pliers have about as many uses as one can dream up. They are a handy size, they grip exceptionally well, and their configurations allow users to grasp unusually shaped items inside awkwardly confined spaces with little trouble. Assured of a solid grip, you can use these tools to unhook small springs, pull cotter pins, anchor unsecured items while tightening fasteners, and a host of other tasks. The jaw gap is adjusted to fit various-sized objects by twisting a knurled screw at the base of one handle. The other handle features a release lever, which is activated by simply depressing it. Use caution when applying these tools' pressure grip, as their strong jaw teeth could mark up or bite surface finishes. If need be, place a heavy cloth between jaws and objects to be secured in order to avoid needless blemishes.

According to American Tool Companies, this CHESCO molded fold-up hex key set is the first to feature a lightweight rugged case made of tough high-tech resin. Its unique ergonomic design fits hands snugly and comfortably for the best grip and maneuverability. Steel hex keys are made from heat-treated steel alloy and are finished in black oxide. The keys open from either the top or the bottom for ease of access and rotate 270 degrees or more while maintaining a steady position at almost any angle. American-calibrated sets include nine sizes, from 5/64in to 1/4in. Units are also available in metric and TORX sizes.

Kent-Moore

Kent-Moore is the special tool supplier for GM, Nissan, Hyundai, Isuzu, and other miscellaneous smaller customers. Although this company is primarily a direct mail-order business, some distribution is made through mobile distributors. The Kent-Moore product line includes too many items to list here, but you will receive free catalogs of its specialty items by calling the company's toll-free telephone number.

The J 23742 Ball Joint Separator is just one of the many specialty tools offered by Kent-Moore. It is designed for the upper and lower ball joints on all GM rear-wheel-drive vehicles except the F-, P-, and T-cars. Catalogs also include listings for items like valve spring testers, brake testers, digital multimeters, valve guide seal installers, harmonic balancer holders, clutch plate pullers, and a great deal more.

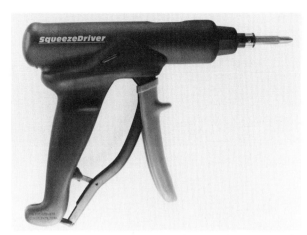

A 1988 *Popular Science* Tool Award winner, the SqueezeDriver might be just what you require when away from your shop or garage and in need of a high-speed screwdriver, powerful ratchet driver, or light-duty drill. It typically develops an average of 200 revolutions per minute (rpm) and can attain a maximum in excess of 350rpm. An easy squeeze delivers up to 27lb-in of torque to break loose screws or drive them into selected surfaces. The SqueezeDriver is reversible and can also be rotated like a wrench for added torque needs. Standard ¼in hex bits are accommodated, and the unit has a maximum ratchet torque mode of 140lb-in. Optional accessories include a twelve-piece drive bit set, a keyless drill chuck, and a thirteen-piece high-speed steel drill bit set sized from ¹⁄₁₆in to ¼in.

Intermark World Products

Intermark World Products markets a wide variety of products for a host of enterprising companies. Among some hand tools, this company carries lighting equipment and specialty aftermarket accessories for automotive applications. Catalogs and information sheets are available by contacting the company.

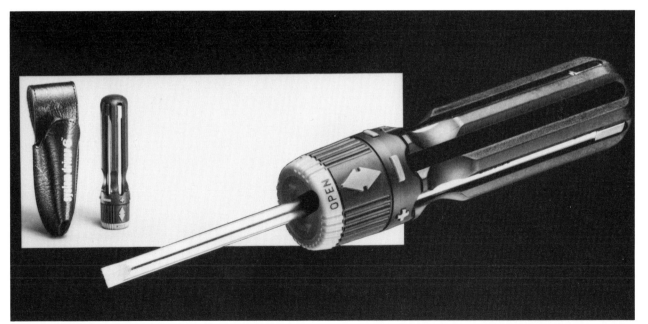

The Intermark System Driver 6 general-purpose screwdriver is perfect for part-time do-it-yourself auto maintenance buffs or as a handy attribute inside trunk toolboxes or glove compartments. Six screwdriver blades fit inside the handle to make this tool a compact storage item. A magnetic chuck locks selected blades in place once they are inserted for actual use. You do not totally remove the blades from the handle when you want to use one. Instead, you twist a retaining ring located at the base of the handle until the indicator arrow points to the desired blade. You then slip that blade out as far as possible, move it to the center of the tool, and push it into the magnetic chuck until you hear a click. Once the blade is properly positioned, you move the retainer ring to the locked position. Symbols on the handle indicate at which point each of six blades is stored. Users can select from both small- and medium-sized slotted, Phillips, and TORX blades.

P.C.S.

P.C.S. manufactures and distributes engine testing stands and other automobile tools and equipment. Brochures describing the company's products are available upon request. Some of the firm's products are also offered through Bill Mitchell Hardcore Racing and Summit Racing Equipment.

The P.C.S. telescopic Camshaft Installation Tool is used for gently guiding camshafts into engines. As cams reach farther and farther into engines, the ability to maintain their position becomes compromised. This tool helps users better control camshafts to avoid banging their sharp lobe ends against soft metal cam bearings. Gouged bearings will generally result in a loss of engine oil pressure, which would then require an engine teardown for cam bearing replacement. Complete with adapters, this tool will fit onto most domestic camshafts.

Harbor Freight Tools

Harbor Freight Tools is a catalog sales company that deals in a wide variety of hand and power tools, industrial equipment, and other automotive repair and maintenance accessories. It carries a number of name brand items and offers free catalogs to customers on its current mailing list, as well as those who contact the company by phone or letter. If you need a tool in a hurry and it is ordered early enough, Harbor Freight will ship it Next-Day Delivery. Once again, this company's catalog contains far too many entries to include them all here. For more information and acquisition of its catalog, call Harbor Freight at its toll-free number.

Art Wentworth is turning the saddle on this 2$\frac{1}{4}$ Ton Hydraulic Jack from Harbor Freight Tools in preparation for raising the front end of Bill O'Brien's 1939 classic Chevrolet four-door sedan. This heavy-duty floor jack weighs in at 69 pounds (lb). Lowered, the saddle goes down to just 5in. Fully raised, it reaches up to 19$\frac{1}{4}$in. The unit features heavy-gauge welded construction, and the arm is reinforced. Just a twist of the handle is all it takes to set up this jack in a lifting or lowering mode. Smaller units are available, but their limitations might prove frustrating when trying to raise heavy vehicles, especially those of yesteryear equipped with lots of heavy-duty panels and suspension members. Note: *Never* rely solely upon any jack to hold a raised automobile securely while you are working underneath it; *always* stabilize vehicles with sturdy jack stands strategically placed on frame members or axles, before crawling or "creeping" under them.

Chapter 2

Power and Pneumatic Tools

The arms, wrists, and hands of those who work on cars and trucks provide lots of power to wrenches, ratchets, screwdrivers, pliers, and other hand tools. For pneumatic volume, one might surmise that a few choice words screamed out every now and again could vaguely qualify as compressed air power—or rather, hot air motivation. Be that as it may; either you understand the need to voice frustrations or you don't. To those of us who have occasionally tried and tried to make certain auto things fit and operate properly only to fail time and time again, this statement is certainly understandable.

Do-it-yourself automobile restorers and repair people are all too familiar with the frustrations and complexities that surround the world of automotive repair. How many times have we begged for a certain tool that would make our jobs easier? Have you ever promised yourself that before you started your next restoration project, you would invent and build a specific tool to make this or that job go much easier and faster? Only to find yourself stuck in the same dilemma a few months later without it?

Fortunately, as we go about the tasks of making our favorite rides run like race cars, look like centerfold masterpieces, and operate like well-oiled, treasured chariots, a number of companies are valiantly inventing, building, and marketing power and pneumatic tools and equipment that can make our automotive restoration and repair jobs a lot easier.

Not that many years ago, who would have dreamed that a tool could actually turn a screw or fasten a nut under its own battery power while you just held it steady with a firm grip? How much time do you think it took your grandfather to grind down a weld with a coachman's file? Can you imagine how much personal energy it took to saw through a section of sheet metal with a hacksaw?

Well, the auto restorers and repair people of this era are fortunate to have a wide variety of power and pneumatic tools at their disposal for the cutting, grinding, and fastening of all sorts of automotive attributes. Not only can one save time by using these implements but one can also be assured of straight cuts, properly torqued fasteners, and quality finish results.

The phrase "power and pneumatic tools" could encompass a great many topics. For this chapter, however, consider the examples of these items that are operated by hand and require no more than a normal household electrical outlet or common air compressor. Featured items will be tools you can afford and put to good use on your treasured project vehicle, regular driver, or show machine.

When trying to decide which air compressor would be best suited for your needs, take time to read the labels on the pneumatic power tools you have or are planning to purchase. They will list minimum cfm and psi requirements that must be met by the corresponding compressor. If a compressor unit is too small, it will not allow air tools to operate at maximum capacities. In addition, you'll find that the motors on smaller units will run constantly, increasing the amount of heat produced and moisture introduced into the air supply. Likewise, small air storage tanks cannot be expected to supply required air demands to high-speed tools, like rotary sanders, which go through high cfm allotments in a hurry. Those who expect to use powerful pneumatic tools on a regular basis should purchase an air compressor with a minimum 5hp rating and 30gal tank. Professional bodyshops rely on minimum 10hp units with 60gal to 100gal storage tanks.

K. O. Lee Company

The K. O. Lee Company has been involved with machinery activities since before the turn of the twentieth century. Through a series of marketing and economical events, this company has flourished as a leader in the field of cutter grinders. Today, the K. O. Lee Company is a major producer of tool and cutter grinders for both the automotive and industrial fields. For auto enthusiasts, look to the K. O. Lee Company for professional equipment when it comes to valve and valve seat grinding.

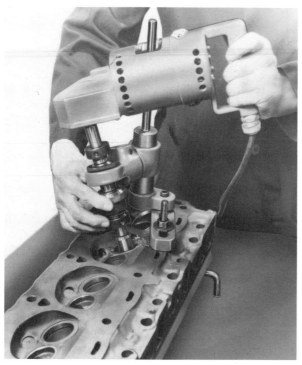

Professional engine rebuilders and serious do-it-yourself restorers prefer to tackle most jobs themselves, to make sure everything is done "right." If you are inclined to set up an automotive workshop with all the right equipment, you'll need valve grinders, refacers, and, as shown here, reseater sets. The K. O. Lee Company can provide you with state-of-the-art equipment for completing jobs correctly the first time. The company's catalog lists plenty of tools, equipment, and accessories to make any job flow smoothly and result in a quality finish.

Dremel

Dremel is well known for its MOTO-TOOL products. These tools are high-speed, handheld rotary devices capable of a wide assortment of small grinding, cutting, polishing, sanding, cleaning, deburring, and other projects. A number of tools are available with various rpm, torque, and optional accessory features, each designed to accommodate specific user needs. Dremel's product line also includes an expansive selection of bits, Flex-Shaft models, stands, engravers, sharpeners, cutting devices, and other accessories. To further complement a series of variable-speed, cordless, and mini MOTO-TOOL units, Dremel manufactures larger products that include a combination disc-belt sander and variable-speed scroll saw.

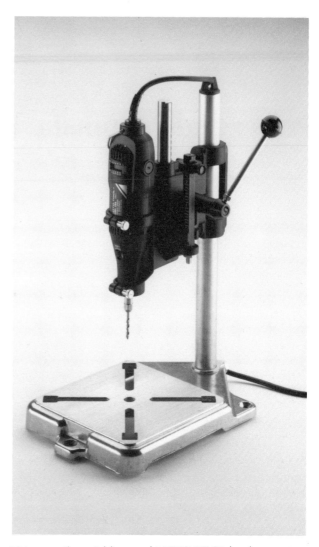

This versatile variable-speed MOTO-TOOL has been set up for drilling in a Dremel optional drill press. It takes only a few minutes to secure a tool into the drill press stand in preparation for precision drilling. A rack-and-pinion feed handle has a calibrated depth shaft, and the 6in-by-6in slotted base easily accommodates hold-down clamps. For intricate polishing, grinding, or sanding work, Dremel also offers MOTO-TOOL holder and base units. With a tool secured in the desired position, operators are able to use both hands to control work pieces—a real plus when sanding or polishing small, awkwardly shaped auto components.

Porter-Cable Corporation

Porter-Cable Corporation produces many different power tools designed for both professionals and do-it-yourselfers and for their diverse needs. Close attention is given to the latest technology with regard to improved power supplies for products. Emphasis is placed on the tool design characteristics that will best accommodate user requirements. This means, among other things, that tool weight distribution is frequently balanced in ways to help work be accomplished easier, faster, and with less need for a lot of operator muscle.

Porter-Cable's 12volt MAGNEQUENCH ³/₈in cordless driver-drill is available in both keyless and standard chuck versions. The units are variable speed and reversible. A nickel cadmium battery produces 12 full volts of power. Combined with revolutionary new magnet technology in the motor, its battery pack is able to deliver more work between charges than ever before. Heavy-duty planetary gearing allows these tools to stand up under rugged use. A six-position clutch is standard and provides torque settings of approximately 5 pounds-inches (lb-in), 21lb-in, 27lb-in, 53lb-in, and 70lb-in. Also standard is an equipment list that includes a one-hour fast charger, #2 Phillips insert bit, operating manual, and heavy-duty steel carrying case that has space for an extra battery pack and commonly used bits. Porter-Cable's unique Thrust-Line grip allows a user to place his hand directly behind the chuck for straighter and more accurate drilling and fastening.

The basic Porter-Cable vertical power tool can be outfitted with attachments that make it a versatile polisher, disc sander, or grinder. Other attachments are also available for a variety of do-it-yourself projects. The motor-over-pad design shown here places the motor's weight directly over work surfaces to make sanding easier and faster. This design also improves control and balance. This tool features a heavy-duty 8ampere (amp) motor and a variable-speed range of 3500rpm to 4500rpm. Helical gears offer quiet operation and ensure long tool life. The heavy-duty rubber-insulated power cord is 10 feet (ft) long. Side handles are adjustable and can be mounted on either side of the tool to accommodate both left- and right-handed operators. A ⁵/₈in-11 spindle accepts all standard sanding accessories.

Makita U.S.A.

Makita U.S.A. has seven regional office-distribution centers, forty-seven factory service centers, and over 260 authorized service centers throughout the United States that provide complete, prompt, and efficient service for its numerous power tools and accessories. The *Makita Industrial Quality Power Tool* catalog is chock-full of various products, including lots of handy accessories. It also carries the names, locations, and telephone numbers of authorized service centers throughout the country. To locate the one nearest you, look in your Yellow Pages under the heading for electric tools.

The Makita Model 6720DW Cordless Screwdriver is equipped with a 150rpm high-tech motor designed to drive a variety of screw sizes. It has an automatic locking feature that enables it to be used as a manual screwdriver, too. The slide on-off switch complements a comfortable hand grip area to assist one-handed control maneuvers. Three hours is all it takes to recharge the built-in 2.4volt battery, and that charge is generally good enough for up to 220 uses. Driver bits are easy to insert and remove. An electric brake stops bits fast to help reduce the chances of screw head stripping. Standard packages include the tool, a charger, and a double-ended combination bit.

Makita's slim-line cordless ratchet is ideal for use in awkward or hard-to-reach spaces. The Model 6912DW Cordless Ratchet is compact and light, weighing in at only 1.9lb. Users can expect to get 400rpm out of these units, with a torque range of up to 2.7lb-ft while the tool is running. Instead of operating a switch to reverse tool revolutions, users simply flip the unit over. Along with the ratchet, packages include a battery, charger, and socket adapter. To save money, you could purchase tools without a battery and charger and just use a battery and charger from other cordless Makita products currently in your shop or garage, as numerous Makita cordless tools utilize the same 7.2volt direct current (DC) battery units.

Auto restoration and repair efforts often present technicians with puzzling problems, especially when it comes to the ability to fit certain tools into limited-access areas. Makita's compact DA3000R $^3/_8$in Angle Drill may be just the tool you need for drilling holes into deep panel attributes or engine compartment spaces. It is reversible and operates at variable speeds up to 1400rpm. Since it weighs only 3.5lb, users are generally able to control the tool with one hand in really tight spots. The motor housing grip and paddle switch are convenient and comfortable; revolution speed is controlled by the paddle switch. This model comes standard with a heavy-duty chuck and chuck key.

Makita Model 9005B Angle Grinder units are powerful 5in grinders. With optional accessories, these power tools can also double as high-performance sanders. A 9.4amp motor is capable of producing up to 10,000rpm, and tool weight is low at just 6.6lb. This model utilizes a standard $^5/_8$in-11 UNC spindle. The side handle can be secured on either side of the unit, a shaft lock assists in changing wheels, and a lock-on button allows for continuous use without strain. Items included in the standard equipment package are a grinding wheel, wheel guard, inner flange, locknut, wrench, and handle.

Designed for use in tight spaces, the Black and Decker #6016 Stubby ³/₈in Right Angle Drill is compact and powerful. It measures only 3³/₄in from its top to its chuck tip, and the powerful 3.2amp motor produces 1650rpm. Double gear reduction increases the unit's torque capability, and ball bearing construction helps to prolong years of trouble-free service. A paddle switch is conveniently integrated into the design to make the tool's operation more maneuverable. This heavy-duty model weighs 3.25lb and comes with an 8ft power cord, chuck key, and chuck key holder.

Black and Decker

Black and Decker power tools have assisted thousands of do-it-yourselfers involved with myriad automotive restoration and repair projects. Used according to their design, power tools go a long way toward making work and hobby endeavors safe and smoother-flowing operations. This company is aware of the vastly different needs for its products. Standard-duty tools are manufactured to provide specific types of service for occasional users, with the appeal of lower unit prices. For those who require powerful and rugged power tools for use on a daily basis, heavy-duty models are available at slightly higher prices.

The standard-duty ¹/₄in Cordless Ratchet from Black and Decker spins nuts and bolts on and off at 120rpm. In the battery operating mode, it will produce torque of up to 50lb-in. Use it as a manual ratchet and you can obtain up to 50lb-ft of torque. The tool head rotates 350 degrees for easy access and can also be utilized as a right-angle screwdriver. Included in the standard equipment package are an impact protection sleeve; bench-or-wall–mount charger; ¹/₄in-square-to-¹/₄in-hex screwdriver bit adapter; T15 and T20 TORX screwdriver bits; #1, #2, and #3 Phillips bits; and #5-6 and #8-10 slotted screwdriver bits.

Sears Roebuck and Company

To automotive do-it-yourselfers and professionals alike, Sears is probably most commonly known for its Craftsman brand of hand tools and power equipment. Craftsman hand tools carry lifetime warranties; if they break, just bring them into any Sears store and retrieve a new tool on the spot with no questions asked. Power tools and other equipment do not enjoy this same kind of warranty, and their coverage is limited to specific time periods. Sears catalogs introduce customers to an ever-expanding product line that features everything from screwdrivers and wrench sets to battery chargers and drill presses. Call the company's toll-free number to order the *Sears Power and Hand Tool Catalog.*

Pneumatic (compressed air–powered) tools and equipment offer users a convenient means to achieve many mechanical work projects, autobody repair procedures, and general maintenance endeavors. In lieu of constantly plugging extension cords into and unplugging them from electrical power tool cords, you can quickly and conveniently connect and disconnect a single air hose at pneumatic tool handles. Air compressors are rated in a few different ways. Horse-power (hp), cubic feet per minute (cfm), pounds per square inch (psi), and storage tank gallon sizes are mixed and matched to provide different levels of overall service. This Craftsman Air Compressor has a 5hp rating and is outfitted with a 30gal storage tank. Notice that the unit requires a 240volt power source. This combination will provide 12cfm at 40psi or 10cfm at 90psi. A maximum of 125psi can be developed.

William K. Westley Company

The William K. Westley Company is known for high-performance and creative chemistry products. It manufactures a full line of cleaners, polishes, conditioners, catalysts, and starters—tune-ups for a wide variety of industrial applications.

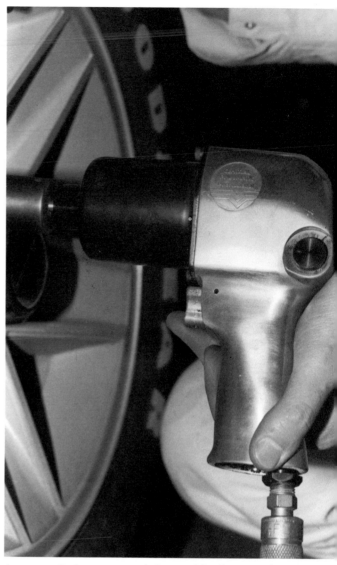

Once you have your air compressor set up and your air tools equipped with a proper air hose coupling, most of your pneumatic power implements will require daily lubrication, as indicated at the base of both the impact wrench and rotary sander shown here. Spinning around at very high rpm speeds or under high torque pressure creates a great deal of friction and associated heat. Dirt- or debris-clogged mechanisms could easily and quickly render tools useless. The Westley B'laster 404 Air-Tool Oil/Conditioner is specially formulated to restore and prolong the working life of power air tools. This product instantly cleans and lubricates tools. It also inhibits rust and increases rpm speeds while tools are in use. Simply spray B'Laster 404 into the air inlet openings of tools to remove calcium build-up, varnish, sludge, and water, to begin immediately restoring used tools and preserving the life of new ones.

Harbor Freight Tools

Harbor Freight Tools catalogs feature a large inventory of name brand power and pneumatic tools and equipment for a multitude of jobs and do-it-yourself endeavors. Many tools are highlighted with accessory options to give customers the opportunity to turn some products into multiple-function units.

A pneumatic impact wrench is a real back saver when it comes to loosening lug nuts, suspension bolts, and other large-caliber fasteners. The Chicago Pneumatic $\frac{1}{2}$in Square Drive Air Impact Wrench from Harbor Freight Tools can develop an incredible 350lb-ft of torque, and its patented twin regulator allows operators to select from any of five power ranges in either forward or reverse. A steel nose hammer case and permanently lubricated air motor help to make this a rugged, heavy-duty, and reliable tool. It operates at 90psi and requires an air source of 4cfm. In a free speed mode, it can develop 5800rpm. You should supply this unit with at least a $\frac{3}{8}$in-diameter air hose, and the air inlet coupling connection is $\frac{1}{4}$in NPT.

HTP America

HTP America started out as strictly a welding machine manufacturer and supplier. Over the years, this company has broadened its sights, and it now caters to both professional and do-it-yourself auto restorers and repair people—from street and hot rodders to those who just like to tinker occasionally and more serious automobile restorers. Along with a wide selection of metal–inert gas (MIG) welders geared toward automotive use, HTP also offers a good selection of plasma cutters, autobody tools, and accessories. HTP builds, services, and uses its own welders. Living up to a commitment of superior customer service, the firm offers a toll-free telephone number that will put customers in contact with staff who can offer expert advice and recommendations with regard to welding or other tasks that employ HTP products.

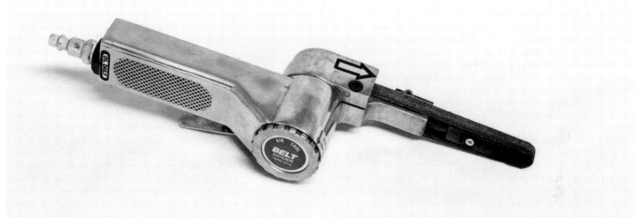

The HTP #90140 Belt Sander is a handy item. Its narrow belt is perfect for sanding in corners or along small parts. Use this pneumatic tool to port cylinder heads, grind down inside corner welds, remove unsightly casting blemishes, and do a lot more. Sanding belts are $3/8$in wide and come in grits that range from 36 (very coarse) to 400 (very fine), with many grits in between. Belts can be changed in seconds, thanks to a simple "quick-change" belt guide design. The adjustable belt guide rotates a full 160 degrees to help users reach out-of-the-way tight spots. In corners, use the nose for plenty of sanding power. On flat surfaces, lay the belt down to take advantage of its length.

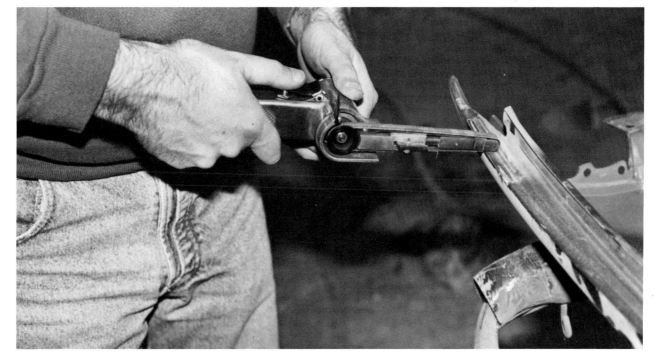

The Eastwood Company

The Eastwood Company maintains a large inventory of the various power tools generally needed for all types of automotive repair and restoration endeavors. This mail-order company directs its full attention strictly to a market of automotive enthusiasts and professionals. Each catalog is filled with tools and equipment designed to make your auto projects flow easier and result in professional-looking finishes.

Cutting through sheet metal, rusty exhaust clamps, frozen bumper bolts, and steel rods up to ³/₄in thick is easy for the Eastwood Utility Cut-Off Tool. An abrasive wheel spins around at 20,000rpm for powerful cutting strength. Its clear plastic cover helps to divert sparks and metal debris away from users, although you should still wear a full face shield and heavy-duty gloves when operating this tool. The air inlet coupling connection is a standard ¹/₄in NPT. The tool operates at 90psi and requires an air supply of 4cfm. A minimum 1hp air compressor should be sufficient to keep this tool operating as long as needed. Abrasive wheel replacements are available in packages of either six or twenty-five.

Operating the Utility Cut-Off Tool from Eastwood does not necessarily require a great deal of instruction, although users need some practice to become confidently familiar with the tool's feel and handling traits. To cut out a section of sheet metal, as Dan Mycon is doing along this fuel filler housing on an otherwise-crumpled pickup truck bed, start the tool slowly to initiate a working groove. Then, let the tool do the cutting work as you steadily guide it along a predetermined path; you do not need to force it into the metal. To achieve straight cuts, many conscientious technicians lay down a strip of masking tape to mark cutting paths. Notice that Mycon is wearing a full face shield and heavy-duty work gloves. Also note the quantity of sparks created by this tool's cutting action and how far those sparks are thrown out.

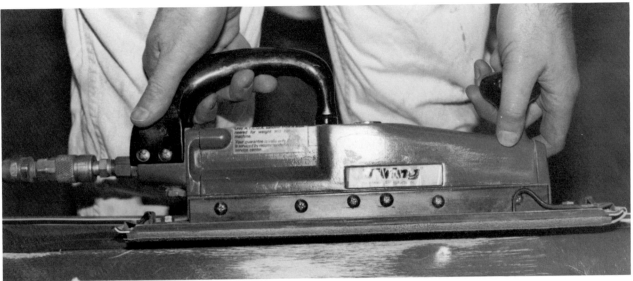

Air pressure powers the body of the Dual Piston Filer/Sander. It takes 90psi for sanding work and 120psi for filing; each maneuver requires 4cfm. Sandpaper sheets are easy to affix to this tool, as are the 14in body files used for smoothing and evening sections of soldered repairs on steel body panels. The tool body is driven in the same direction the tool carrier is moving. This helps to eliminate bucking and chopping. You must keep this tool moving at all times. Allowing it to sit and sand on just one spot will result in grooves or other uneven blemishes on body panels. Coarse-grit sandpaper makes quick work of knocking down initial coats of body filler on flat body panels. Finer-grit sandpaper sheets are more appropriate in preparation for hand block sanding. You should wear a filter mask and eye protection while operating this tool. The mask will prevent sanding dust from infiltrating your respiratory system, and goggles will eliminate the accumulation of dust in your eyes.

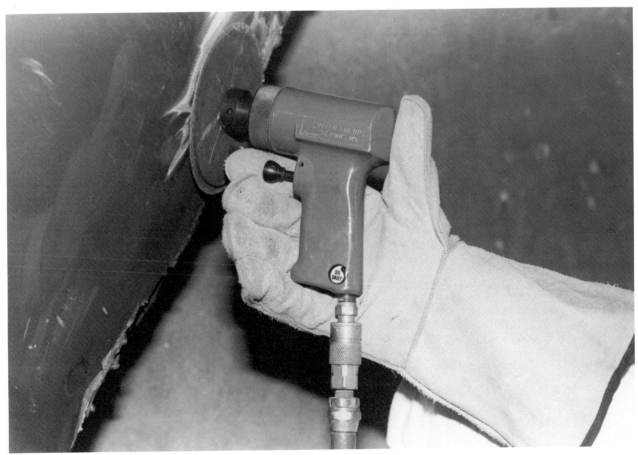

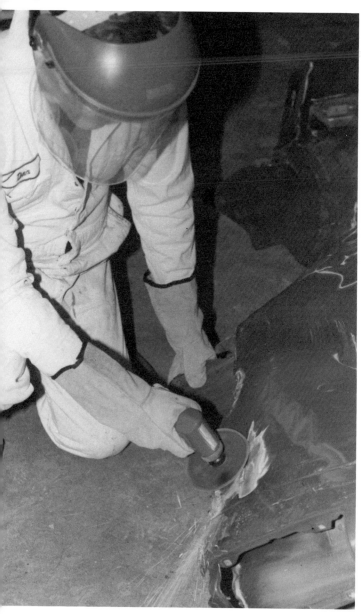

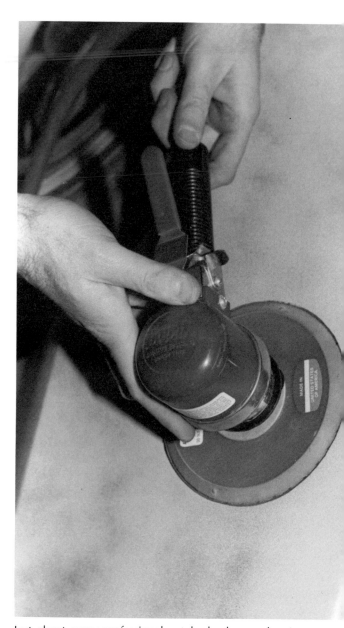

Used with the correct-grit sanding disc, the High Speed Rotary Sander from Eastwood can knock down welding beads, flatten nibs, and remove paint layers in short order. This unit spins at speeds up to 20,000rpm with 90psi to 110psi and 4cfm. All–ball bearing construction with a diecast aluminum housing makes it rugged and lightweight. Both 3in and 5in fiber backing pads supplement the tool package. Like other high-speed tools, this one will also throw off showers of sparks when sanding operations entail using coarse discs on metal panels. Therefore, wear a full face shield and gloves. Because the tool operates through abrasive friction, heat will build up on surfaces. This is an important concern when working on the thin body panels of newer automobiles. Too much heat incurred by these panels will cause them to warp. Therefore, limit aggressive sanding maneuvers to short as opposed to prolonged time periods.

Just about every professional autobody shop and serious restorer's garage is equipped with a Dual Action Sander. Often simply referred to as DAs, these pneumatic power tools do an excellent job of smoothing body surfaces in preparation for paint. This model can be adjusted to operate strictly in a 10,000rpm rotating sander mode or set up for random orbital (jitterbug) dual-action maneuvers. Dual action means the pad moves back and forth, up and down, and sideways concentrically and randomly. At first, users may think the pad is not moving at all because it is not aggressively spinning. These powerful tools will sand away a lot of material in a hurry while in the DA mode, however, even though you may not believe the pad is moving enough. In reality, pads do move around but in short random motions that are difficult to perceive. Various sanding disc grits are required for progressive sanding stages as body panels become smoother. The 80-grit sandpaper discs will initially knock down a lot of material to help flatten panels. Plan to eventually graduate to 120-, 240-, 360-, and 400-grit discs in preparing panels for paint.

The Carbide Burr Set used on die grinders includes a tree-shaped unit that is 3in long, a ¼in-by-2in cylindrical model, a pointed burr measuring 3in long, and a 2¾in round nose cylinder. These superhard carbide burrs are capable of grinding weld beads, shaping metal parts, smoothing cast-ings, and porting cylinder heads. Metal chips will fly off of these burrs, so you must wear a full face shield or goggles for eye protection. Likewise, you should wear gloves to prevent sliver punctures on hands and fingers. The carrying case shown here is handy and comes as part of this set.

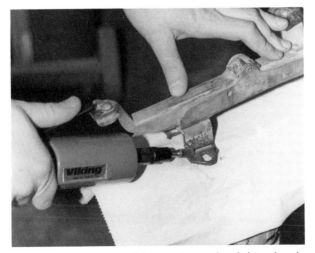

The Die Grinder is used for porting and polishing heads, manifolds, and other metal components. Here, Mycon uses a carbide burr to smooth a flange on a seat support bracket for his 1948 Chevy. A number of different tips can be used with die grinders, from carbide burrs and abrasive rolls to polishing cones and tapered rasps. This unit has a free speed of 20,000rpm. Its direct drive design and ¼in collet make this die grinder a versatile power tool. The trigger paddle located on top of the housing regulates the speed at which the motor spins. Your air compressor needs to deliver 90psi and 4cfm to make the tool operate at capacity.

Snap-on Tools Corporation

The Snap-on Tools Corporation is well-known for its supply of quality automotive tools and equipment. The company relies on locally based dealers to service professional automotive repair, autobody, and paint facilities through mobile vans that make scheduled stops on a regular basis. Sales are also made to nonprofessionals. Contact your local dealer by calling the number listed in your Yellow Pages or by writing to the company's headquarters address.

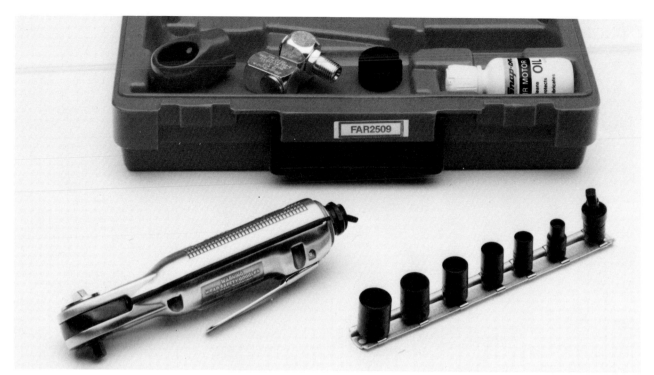

Snap-on's FAR25 ¼in Square Drive Air Ratchet is a tough tool with lots of versatility. Its compact size is perfect for work under instrument panels and in other close quarters with hard-to-reach small fasteners that are nearly impossible to loosen or tighten with standard ratchets or wrenches. Air exhaust is vented out the back of this tool away from the operator. The ratchet weighs just slightly over a pound, is only 6¾in long, and boasts a trim 1¹³/₃₂in diameter. The easy-to-operate paddle trigger regulates ratchet head speed and power. Only 1.4cfm are required at 90psi. The kit comes standard with a ¼in impact swivel, an air line swivel, a case with a handle, and six ¼in-drive impact sockets in sizes of ¼in, ⁵/₁₆in, ³/₈in, ⁷/₁₆in, ½in, and ⁹/₁₆in.

Large ½in-drive air impact wrenches are sometimes too big for engine maintenance and other vehicle repair or restoration chores. That's why Snap-on offers this ³/₈in Drive Impact Wrench, complete with the vinyl boot shown here. A full-size handle provides a firm, comfortable grip along with a precision variable-speed trigger control. The unit provides from 30lb-ft to 135lb-ft of torque. A forward-reverse lever is located at the back of the tool for easy thumb operation. As with any impact wrench, plan to use only sockets designated for high-impact situations. Sockets not designed for this type of operation may split, crack, or chip under high-pressure applications.

Chapter 3

Testing and Metering Equipment

One could regard the category of testing and metering equipment as one including anything from tire pressure gauges to state-of-the-art diagnostic machines for engines and computers. Many companies produce a huge array of various testing and metering devices all designed to somehow make your car or truck run smoother, faster, or more economically.

When looking through numerous catalogs of automotive testing and metering equipment, you'll discover lots of handy items engineered to calibrate thicknesses, tolerances, tensile strength, atmospheric pressure relationships, gaseous mixtures, electrical flow, and so on. It is not always easy to decide which types of testing or metering devices should become permanent attributes in the drawers of your tool chest. Nor is it simple to choose which products offer the most advantageous and versatile performance features for your overall needs.

Cars and trucks are manufactured today in such a way that specialized computers are required for specific engine calibrations and accessory maintenance. It can become quite confusing. In fact, professional mechanics are virtually inundated with hundreds of thousands of pages of reports, statistics, and technical bulletins each year, all seemingly attempting to assist them in their troubleshooting endeavors.

Your need for testing and metering tools and equipment depends upon your level of involvement in automobile service, repair, and restoration, as well as your bank account. Some measuring and diagnostic devices are economical, whereas others are priced for professional shops that rely on consistent customer business in order to justify and cover overhead costs. The items discussed in this chapter are just a small sampling of what is available through the manufacturers presented. Call or write for catalogs and additional information as your needs warrant.

Neward Enterprises

Neward Enterprises manufactures and distributes a full line of MITYVAC hand-held vacuum pumps. These tools are used for a variety of testing chores, as well as transferring fluids from one storage unit to another and performing other tasks. Call or write for a full list and description of the company's products.

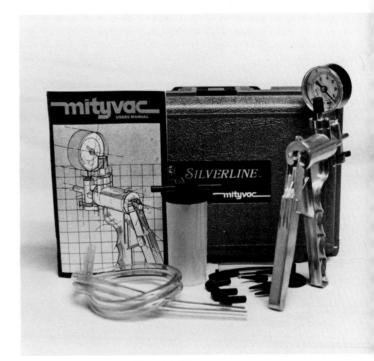

The Silverline MITYVAC hand-held vacuum pump can serve a variety of automotive needs. It is an accurate measuring device for vacuum pumps, hose lines, and control valves but can also be set up to check the condition of seals and to bleed brake lines. The user's manual is vital. It contains over 100 pages of information, directions, and instructions on how to use this tool. It covers, among other topics, diagnosing engine conditions, fuel systems, ignition components, emission controls, automatic transmissions, brakes, and various automotive vacuum reservoirs. Details even include specifications for testing certain auto makes and models.

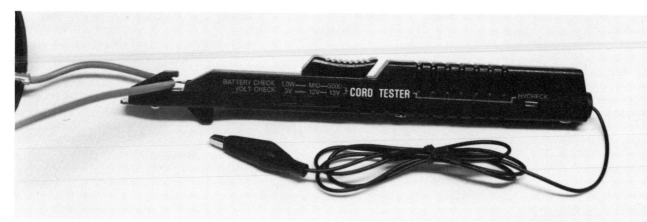

You can test 12volt electrical systems in seconds with the Auto Cord Tester from Harbor Freight Tools. A slim, sharp probe is moved by way of a thumb slide switch to penetrate wiring insulation and make contact with actual electrical wires. Instructions included with the unit are clear and concise. A small light at the rear of the device indicates power or no power, saving you time in chasing down hot wires and wires with no current. This inexpensive tool is also outfitted to test batteries. A metal prong on the tool's nose is used to make contact with the battery terminal, and three lights indicate low (3 volt), medium (12 volt), or good (13volt) battery status.

Pro Motorcar Products

Pro Motorcar Products (PMP) develops and distributes unique automotive gauges and selected repair kits. Simplicity of design and realistic price structures are prevalent prerequisites. Geared for both professional and serious auto enthusiasts, this company's products make for worthwhile investments. More information is available upon request.

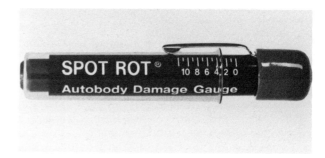

Harbor Freight Tools

To complement its inventory of hand tools, power tools, and other products, Harbor Freight Tools offers selections of numerous testing and metering devices. In the company's catalog, you will find items like digital tire pressure gauges, circuit testers, electronic digital calipers, and more.

The SPOT ROT Autobody Damage Gauge is a simple yet accurate measuring device. It is used to determine how much actual metal exists under layers of paint. A sturdy magnet located inside the device will initially grab hold of base metal. As the unit is gently pulled away from the surface, this magnet will stay affixed, and its clear plastic cover will remain with it. When tension becomes too great to allow the magnet to maintain its hold, the tool breaks loose from the surface. The clear plastic cover, however, will not move, allowing its rear raised lip to remain stationary in order for the operator to determine its calibration indication. Instructions included with the gauge describe which settings alert one to the presence of rust or body filler lurking under paint. This tool is ideal for those in the market for solid used automobiles, as it can detect body panel areas that have been repaired with body fillers or that suffer rust or corrosion under seemingly good paint.

PMP's PRO GAUGE Paint Measuring Gauge operates on a principle that is somewhat similar to that of its partner, the SPOT ROT. A magnet located inside the device makes contact with base metal on automotive body panels. The tool is pulled away from the surface until this magnet breaks contact. Calibrations on the magnet indicate how thick the paint is on selected body panels. Again, instructions offer concise information about paint thickness and the ability to repaint or the need to strip panels to bare metal before painting. Too much paint on body panels will lead to problems with checking, crazing, and other dilemmas. Although one may think that painting over existing paint will result in decent finishes, too many paint layers will work against themselves to render jobs unsatisfactory or heavily marred. This tool is ideal for those contemplating the purchase of a used car with a mediocre paint finish. Within seconds, they will know whether a simple repaint job will suffice or if the vehicle will require a complete paint stripping before painting.

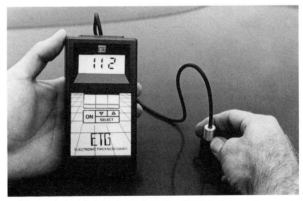

PMP's Electronic Thickness Gauge (ETG) is an electronic gauge that uses microprocessor technology to measure nonferrous coatings—including all metallic paints and non-magnetic platings—on ferrous (steel) substrates. In other words, it measures the depth of paint and undercoat materials down to the body panel surfaces. The device's circuitry measures to 0.00001in and automatically rounds off to 0.0001in for a stable digital display. A slightly more expensive counterpart has attributes that enable it to print out a hard copy display using your International Business Machines–(IBM-) compatible computer and printer. Along with this unit's ease of operation, which requires just three buttons, the cost is far below comparable competitors' products. This is a useful tool for professional auto painters and those seriously involved with automotive restorations and painting needs.

The Eastwood Company

The Eastwood Company prides itself in an inventory of tools and equipment designed for do-it-yourself auto restorers and professionals alike. Every item in its catalog has been fieldtested in its own automotive workshop.

Equipped with test leads, a protective case, and an informative manual, the Digital Engine Analyzer from Eastwood will accurately read dwell angles; conduct volt-ohm functions; check plug wire resistance, battery capacities, and charging system outputs; test alternator components; and more. The large liquid crystal display (LCD) read-out is much more accurate than needle-type meters and easier to read, too. An inductive pickup quickly clips around a spark plug wire for easy tachometer readings up to 10,000rpm. The unit is calibrated and designed to read four-, six-, and eight-cylinder engines with just the flip of a switch. It is also designed to read both live and dead electrical circuits.

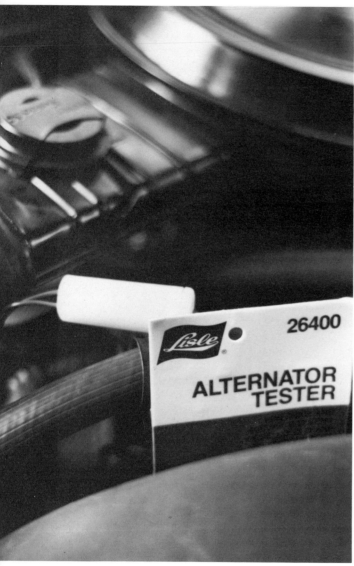

Simplicity is something that auto enthusiasts often find hard to believe, since automobiles have become such complex machines. The Alternator Tester, however, from Eastwood may prove to be both a simple device and a worthwhile tool. It is designed for use on Delco 10 SI and 12 SI alternators to pinpoint operational problems with alternators or voltage regulators or both. Instructions show users how to hook up and decipher the device to determine if electrical current is flowing correctly or not. Basically, a light bulb inside the plastic case lights up or remains idle depending upon which test is underway. An electrical fitting on the end of the unit's wires is set up to plug directly into a connection on Delco alternator units.

Autotronic Controls Corporation

Government regulations relating to environmental and fuel consumption criteria have strained engine building and modifying efforts through restrictions in emissions and mandatory fuel economy standards. Multiple Spark Discharge (MSD) Ignition has met those restrictive regulations head-on with a wide variety of ignition packages designed to maximize combustion on all sorts of automotive vehicles. The company's catalog designates which products are suited for particular vehicles, including specialized off-road and racing machines. In addition, MSD Ignition tells customers which products are street legal in all states and which carry the approval of the California Air Resources Board (CARB). Those products are designated with a CARB Executive Order Number, which the Environmental Protection Agency (EPA) accepts as meeting the requirements of its Memorandum 1A and the Clean Air Act amendments of 1990.

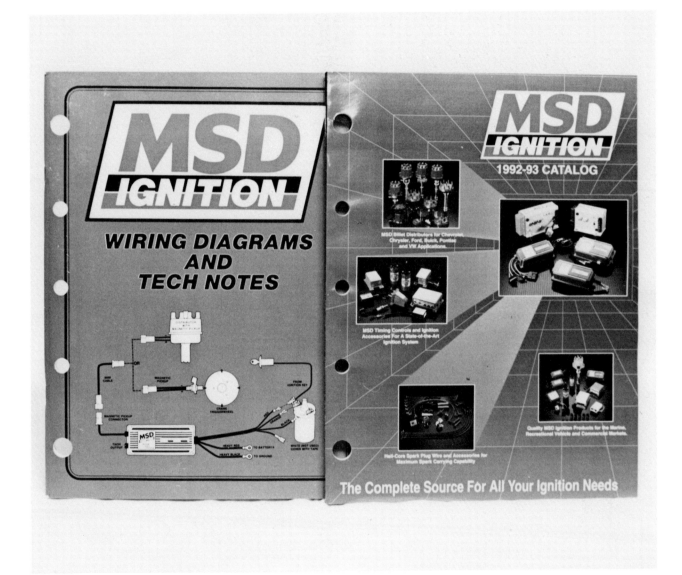

These MSD Ignition publications are filled with a great deal of information. In *Wiring Diagrams and Tech Notes,* you will find instructions on how to wire in MSD Ignition products, including directions for specific auto makes like Ford, GM, and Chrysler. It also includes compatibility charts for various coils and descriptions and information about rotor phasing, MSD products and batteries, radio noise, and how to use a magnetic pickup trigger. The *Parts Catalog* is just as definitive. It offers full product descriptions and details, and performance benefits for ignition products like coils, distributors, monitors, ignition wires, and related accessories.

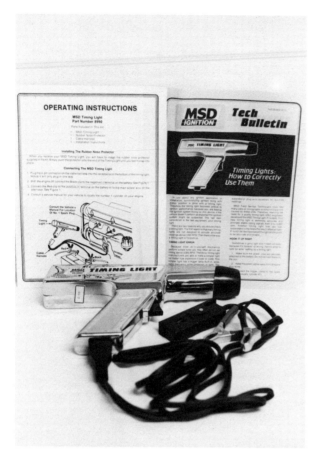

The MSD Timing Light is manufactured with dedicated racers and mechanics in mind. It is a rugged unit that's easy to use and exceptionally accurate. A silicon-controlled rectifier (SCR) provides accurate and stable timing signals from 0rpm to 8000rpm, and the Linear Xenon flash tube and focused Fresnel lens provide light that is bright enough to see in broad daylight. The tool's chrome-plated housing is tough and it's easy to clean, and the durable rubber nose cone helps to protect the Fresnel lens. An inductive pickup is made of metal so that it will not melt if accidentally touched against a hot exhaust header or manifold. The battery clamps are color coded, and the leads are strong enough to resist burns and cuts. These leads are also detachable to make tool storage easier. Timing light packages include detailed operating instructions and an informative tech bulletin.

The MSD Ignition Tester is designed to help users trace ignition problems on four-, six-, and eight-cylinder engines equipped with MSD Ignition products and on many with standard electronic ignition systems. This unit is simply plugged into the magnetic pickup input or points input on an MSD ignition or timing accessory for testing an entire ignition system while it is still on a car and connected. Basically, the unit produces a simulated trigger signal that fires the ignition system as if the engine were running. A special wide-gap clip-on test spark plug is included that connects to the ignition coil wire. This wide-gap plug places a load on the ignition system as if it were spark plugs firing under compression. A weak coil, bad ignition, low battery, or other problems will cause this spark to be weak and unable to jump the gap. Once a problem is recognized through the digital read-out, users can go about tracing the source.

The MSD 3-in-1 Distributor Set Up Tool is used to determine the correct length for the intermediate shafts of oil pumps on engines that have been line bored (a modification that can change the distance between an oil pump and distributor drive). The tool is also instrumental in determining the proper slip collar position on any of MSD's Billet Slip Collar Distributors. Once a rebuilt or modified engine has been assembled, the tool can be used to prime oil pumps and prelube bearings.

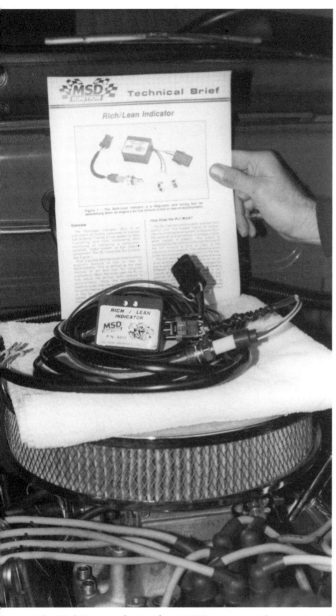

The Rich/Lean Indicator from MSD measures the amount of oxygen in an engine's exhaust. You will need to weld a special $^7/_8$in boss into the exhaust in order to screw in the heated titania oxygen sensor; both parts are included in the kit. Two lights are featured on the testing unit: an illuminated green light indicates an air-fuel mixture that is too rich, and a red light signifies a mixture that is too lean. The point of stoichiometry, which occurs when the air-fuel ratio is 14.7:1, is characterized when the lights switch between green and red. Users can rely upon this tool to check air-fuel mixtures with engines at idle, at wide-open, and under other operating conditions.

The Soft Touch Rev Control unit from MSD can be mounted on a fender apron or firewall. The device is used to limit excessive engine rpm due to missed shifts, broken drivelines, loss of traction, and other dilemmas. In lieu of cutting off all ignition spark at times of dangerous overrevving, as do many rev control devices, the Soft Touch uses computer circuitry to drop one cylinder at a time and then fire that cylinder on the next cycle. This results in smooth action that holds engines at a selected rpm limit without backfires, extreme roughness, or engine damage. Units are supplied with 6000rpm, 7000rpm, and 8000rpm modules. Other modules are available as options. The Soft Touch Rev Control model displayed here is designed for use on standard points ignitions or noncapacitive discharge ignition systems. This means it can be installed on four-, six-, and eight-cylinder engines with GM HEI, or Ford or Chrysler electronic ignitions.

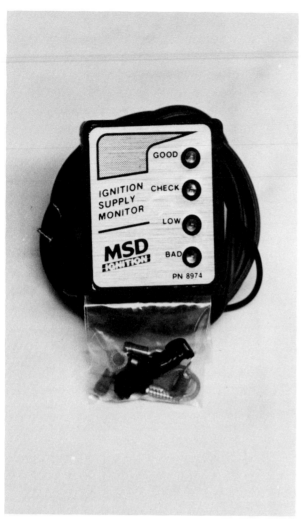

The MSD Ignition Supply Monitor is designed for use on vehicle engines that *do not* have charging systems, like those in race cars. Battery conditions for these engines are critical, as low voltage could drastically affect overall engine performance. The Ignition Supply Monitor measures and averages voltage spikes on MSD 12volt power cables to determine when batteries are good, below normal, low, or bad. This information is valuable in the pits when mechanics attempt to isolate ignition problems that often simply relate to a battery voltage output that is low.

Spark Plug Gapping Pliers from Jacobs Electronics enable mechanics to increase the accuracy of spark plug gapping from 0.025in to 0.085in for any style plug. The tool also provides a simple means to center side electrodes over center electrodes with one easy squeeze. Using this tool on all spark plugs will guarantee that they are all gapped exactly the same. Handles feature a slip-proof coating, and the gapping wheel and spreader are easy to read and manipulate. Users appreciate both not having to fumble with feeler gauges and the precision spark plug gaps this tool consistently delivers.

Jacobs Electronics

Jacobs Electronics is one of the three largest manufacturers of ignition products designed to improve automotive mileage and performance. The company believes that weak ignition systems are the largest single source of engine performance, reliability, and fuel economy problems. A colorful product catalog displays a multitude of ignition parts and accessories, including coils, spark plug wires, computer ignitions, rotors, distributors, and the Nitrous Safety System. Products are available for almost all makes and models of vehicles with four-, six-, and eight-cylinder engines.

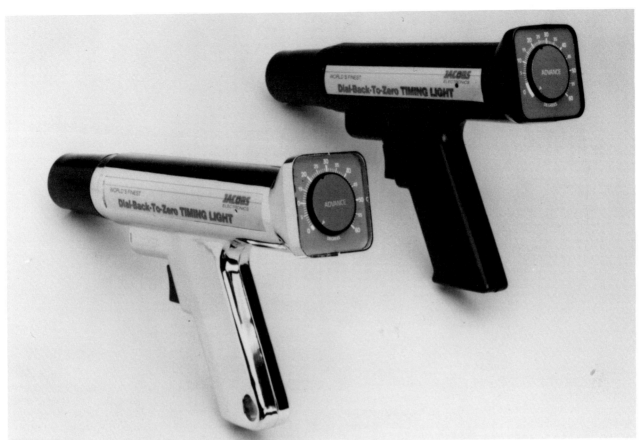

The Jacobs Electronics Dial-Back-To-Zero Timing Light will allow operators to check and curve their own distributors at all rpm without having to remove them. It will also read timing to 60 degrees even when timing marks stop at 10 degrees, time engines accurately to 12,000rpm, and help users find engine timing marks with a built-in spotlight. This unit is designed so that timing can be read off of an engine's large and clearly indicated top dead center (TDC) mark. Various degrees are read off of the back of the timing light. In addition, the tool features a memory trigger for easy one-hand operation and a check light to ensure connections are correctly made.

The OPTO-TIMER can help engines run smoother by stopping pings and eliminating knocks as vehicles are driven up steep hills or suffer ill effects from poor gasoline quality. To operate it, drivers simply turn the dash-mounted dial clockwise to retard timing as they drive. During cold weather or long-distance cruising, timing can be advanced by turning the dial counterclockwise while driving. This unit also features a built-in Rev-Safe rev limiter. Applications are compatible with almost all original equipment of manufacturer (OEM) and aftermarket ignition systems. Complete packages include instructions and all required hardware. Installation can be accomplished in minutes, as the system operates directly off distributors or crank triggers, eliminating the need for an expensive amplifer.

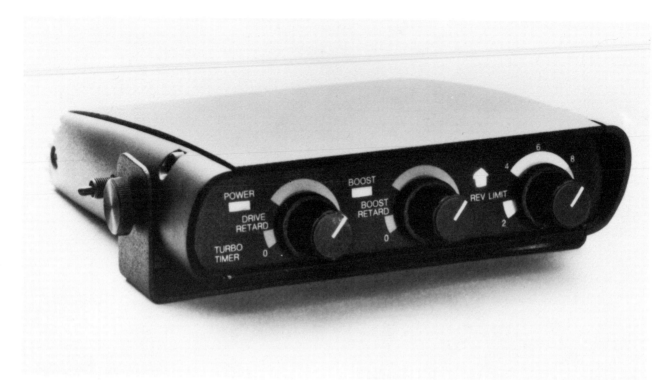

The TURBO-TIMER unit offers the same kind of service as the OPTO-TIMER with an added Turbo Retard mechanism that helps to prevent turbo or blower damage by automatically dialing in the safest maximum-power curve for your engine-vehicle-driving combination when under boost. As soon as the engine comes out of boost, the unit automatically advances to the most responsive curve to maximize fuel mileage and ride smoothness. The TURBO-TIMER offers more power from all forced induction applications, provides better mileage and throttle response when not in boost, and allows more advanced timing for normal driving. It also features a Rev-Safe rev limiter.

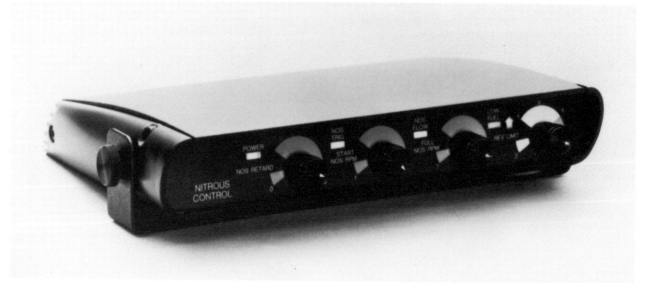

The Jacobs Electronics Nitrous Safety System (NSS) helps to protect engines by immediately sensing when fuel pressure drops below safe levels and then automatically shutting off nitrous flow. It also automatically retards timing when nitrous cuts in. Since nitrous can cause the rpm to jump past safe limits extremely fast, missed shifts, lost traction, broken drivelines, or wheel hop could result in blown engines. To protect against this dilemma, NSS employs a two-step plan.

As the rpm near maximum levels, NSS shuts off nitrous and a built-in Rev-Safe holds the rpm at safe levels. If nitrous is cut in at below minimal rpm, combustion chambers can be over-filled to result in explosions strong enough to bend rods or cave in pistons. NSS can be set to a safe lower-end rpm and will then hold off nitrous injection until that rpm level is reached or exceeded.

Snap-on Tools Corporation

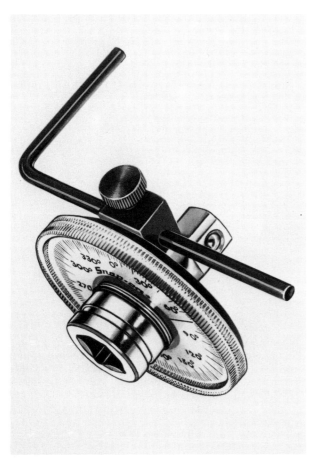

Many vehicle manufacturers now specify certain angles at which fasteners should be tightened after they have been initially torqued. To help mechanics fine-tune such adjustments, Snap-on offers the TA360 Angle Gauge. A large, easy-to-read scale helps take the guesswork out of fastener positioning with marks to 360 degrees in 2-degree increments and 10- to 30-degree intervals.

Snap-on's MT11000 Interface System I is a hand-held modular diagnostic system that features a low-cost set of interchangeable tools for a variety of engine testing needs. The MT1110 Primary Tach/Dwell and MT1120 Volt/Ohm units quickly slide onto the MT1100 Interface Meter for performance testing applications like measuring engine rpm, ignition dwell, and duty cycle functions for electric or electronic switches. The base unit features a digital LCD with large digits, an indicator that warns of a low internal battery, a hold button that freezes live readings on the display, and more. This set comes complete, including a 9volt alkaline battery.

Interchangeable cartridges allow the Snap-on MT2500 Scanner to test all GM, Ford, and Chrysler electronic systems. It provides lists of tests and data read-outs for vehicles in a shop bay or on the road. Along with having a wide-screen display, this unit allows operators to view up to nine data items on the LCD, and four separate light-emitting diode (LED) indicators are easy to screen. Functions are initiated by the use of just two buttons and an exclusive thumb wheel. The Scanner prompts users through a quick selection of key characters from vehicle identification numbers (VINs) in order to arrive at the correct test program for each vehicle being analyzed. As auto manufacturers develop new control programs, new cartridges for the Scanner will be offered.

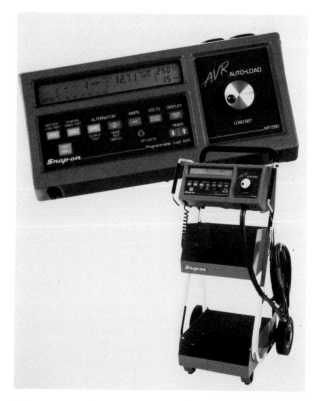

The Snap-on MT1590 Programmable Load AVR delivers easy and accurate testing of starting and charging systems with just the touch of a button. It features an automatic carbon pile load that is selected and applied by a microprocessor. In addition, this testing unit includes an ammeter and a high-impedance voltmeter that enables operators to test batteries, starters, alternators, voltage regulators, and other miscellaneous switches and circuitry. A 1200amp current probe is provided that is capable of testing heavy-duty electrical systems. An optional alternating current (AC) auxiliary supply will power this machine to enable it to test 6volt starting and charging systems and their 6volt batteries.

The Counselor XL Large Screen Digital Oscilloscope is user friendly, was designed with the latest in engineering sophistication, and displays easy-to-follow menu prompts on a large (19in) screen. A Pattern Shift feature repositions primary or secondary waveforms for easier evaluation of their different portions. Pattern Expand enlarges a waveform for closer examination and precise meters-per-second (mps) measurements. Cylinder Shorting power balance tests individual cylinders on waveform screens for primary and secondary ignition circuits.

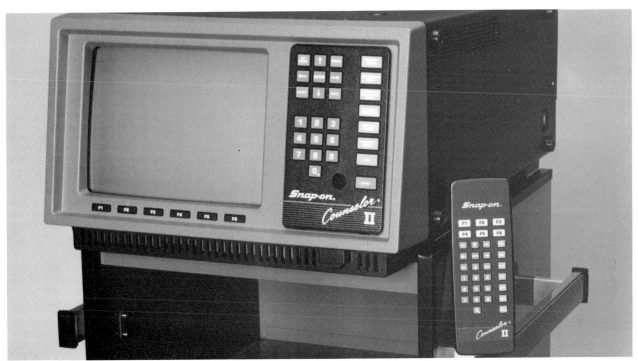

Engine oscilloscopes are designed to analyze engine ignition and electronic systems. The Snap-on Counselor II Digital Oscilloscope is a new-generation model capable of performing seventeen different diagnostic functions. It can analyze virtually any vehicle on the road today, including those with from one to sixteen cylinders and with almost any type of ignition system. Timing lights, timing meters, and other diagnostic devices are easily connected to this unit. Menu screen prompts offer directions that are easy for operators to follow and understand, and a variety of options will allow users to select how they want specific information displayed in order to identify engine trouble sources more readily. To make this tool even more convenient, an optional wireless remote control unit will operate the machine from a distance. The remote is strong enough to operate through glass and has its keys positioned like those on the front panel of the oscilloscope.

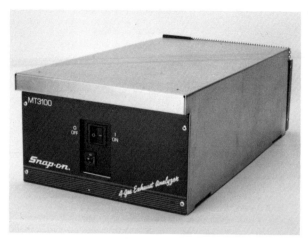

The MT3100 Four-Gas Analyzer is designed to be used with a Snap-on Counselor II Digital Oscilloscope. This analyzer is designed to analyze accurately and provide data on engine emissions. The four gases this unit can analyze are hydrocarbons (HCs), carbon monoxide (CO), carbon dioxide (CO_2), and oxygen (O_2). Information deciphered through this machine is fed to the oscilloscope and then displayed on the screen through use of the Counselor II function keys. The information derived from this analyzer helps mechanics to more accurately adjust air-fuel mixtures and accelerator pumps, as well as determine faulty vacuum lines, leaky power valves, exhaust restrictions, misfiring spark plugs, and more.

Rebuilding engines can sometimes leave mechanics wondering if everything was put together exactly as designed. Generally, this is not known until the engine is installed and started. With the MotherLoad Engine Testing Stand from P.C.S., mechanical problems can be discovered and corrected *before* engines are installed in host vehicles. This test stand is fully adjustable and will accommodate almost any engine, such as V-8s, inlines, Volkswagens, Porsches, and so on. Engines can be positioned as illustrated, placed sideways or at 180 degrees. The unit is portable, offers a weight-bearing capacity of 1,000lb, and moves smoothly on casters rated at 225lb each. When not in use, it can be set on its side and leaned against a wall or support, occupying only 14in of space. Water adapters are included that when properly installed and connected to two regular ³/₄in garden hoses eliminate the need to run fans or fan belts, unless desired. Two models are available: one comes as illustrated, complete with stand, aluminum dash panel, tachometer, oil pressure gauge, water temperature gauge, starter button, on-off switch, throttle cable, tool-battery tray, fuel tank, and water adapters; the other just includes the stand, water adapters, and fuel tank.

Chapter 4

Restoration Tools

Assortments of automobile enthusiasts with varied auto interests may define restoration projects from a full circle of viewpoints. One person could perceive weeks of labor-intensive detailing as a qualified restoration endeavor, whereas others might think of their restoring operations only in the context of full-blown, frame-off, get-down-to-bare-metal, meticulous, and complete supercleaning, repair, rustproofing, paint, and upholstery perfection.

For the most part, though, automobile restoration includes just about any task or series of chores that aims toward eventually bringing a car or truck back to like-new or better condition. That weeks-long detail could classify as a restoration project if paint was polished and rubbed out to a rich luster, upholstery shampooed and trimmed to perfection, engine compartment detailed, motor serviced and tuned up, tires and wheels buffed, trunk space rejuvenated, and so on. Done correctly, meticulous detailing could bring a cosmetically neglected machine back to pristine condition.

On the other hand, an antique or classic vehicle abandoned for decades in an old barn with a leaky roof and no doors, packs of rodents scuttling around, herds of animals scattered about, and flying creatures soaring all over may not respond to detail efforts as well. That car or truck will most likely require extensive repairs, parts replacement, rust removal and patch panels, new cloth, weather stripping, and a lot more.

Complete professional restorations are not limited to just one or two vehicle attributes like engine compartments, bodies, or interiors. Rather, these operations call for the repair and rejuvenation of everything down to the last nut, bolt, cotter pin, and headliner stitch. Those in the business of serious auto restorations realize the amount of time and work these operations require. Typically, customers can expect overall parts and labor to run tens of thousands of dollars, depending upon the year, make, and model in question and the availability of parts replacements.

Do-it-yourselfers can save a great deal of money by restoring cars themselves. This is a feasible option for those with available time, places to work and store parts, the patience to learn a great many automotive repair and rejuvenation techniques, and the ability to read and understand the operating instructions of the tools and equipment that will be used throughout a restoration endeavor.

Steelcrafters

Restoration of older antique and classic automobiles frequently requires extensive work on frames, suspensions, lower body panels, and undercarriage assemblies in general. Steelcrafters helps to make these *undercar* repairs much easier with the use of its BOTTOMS UP Lifts. Entire autobodies can be maneuvered to 90degree angles and complete upside-down positions to accommodate metal repairs, painting, rustproofing, and other rejuvenation projects. A number of other useful restoration pieces of equipment are also available from Steelcrafters. Write or call for additional information on dolly units, chassis carts, rolling racks, and other devices.

Smaller versions of the Mobile Lift from Steelcrafters are the Nonmobile 2,000lb Stands. They have many of the same features as the larger unit, except for capacity and mobility. One model is offered with a fixed-height design, shown here with the Mustang body, and the other is equipped with the same 3ton hydraulic jacks as the 4,000lb model. For restorers on a limited budget with work facilities that will not require a large-capacity car body lift with mobile capability, either of these options may be viable.

The BOTTOMS UP 4,000lb Mobile Lift is outfitted with hydraulic jacks and 17in-diameter wheels to assist easy rolling on most surfaces. The tongue makes it easy to maneuver loaded units by hand or with motorized help. Wheels are inset to reduce stress that could otherwise be forced on car bodies if uprights were to lean in toward them. Stabilizer posts are located on all ends of the unit to function as brakes and also reduce any wobble from tires while aggressive scraping work is underway. The hydraulic jacks used to adjust car bodies can move 38in vertically. With safety pins in place on the uprights, these jacks can be removed for other uses or during sandblasting activities. This lift can be attached to car bodies that rest as low as 10in off the floor, and the telescopic center tongue will accommodate vehicles up to 21ft long. Small casters in the middle of the axles are used to help store the lift. When not in use, stored lifts require only 12 square feet of space.

Two units constitute the MPS Auto Cradle. The Cradle—on the left, with rounded members—attaches to wheel hubs utilizing standard four- or five-bolt plates; special plates can be made to order specifications. The Under Car Carriage—the Y-shaped unit to the right lying flat—is used as a lever bar to rotate heavy car bodies. It may not be needed for small, lightweight "body-only" autos when plenty of helpers are able to provide muscle, although operations are generally safest when it and an engine hoist are used for lifting and manpower is saved for stabilizing needs. The Auto Cradle is designed to handle vehicles weighing up to 4,500 lb. Rotating car bodies to 90 degrees allows restorers to access underbody assemblies and roof structures easily and work on them comfortably.

Black and Decker

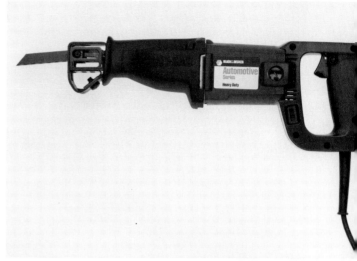

During many major auto restorations, restorers find needs to cut away sheet metal and other items. The #6825 Reciprocating Saw from Black and Decker may be the ideal tool for separating panels, cutting out bad body sections in areas where flame from a torch could be unsafe, and performing a multitude of other sawing tasks on unusually shaped attributes. The tool sports dual-range variable-speed capability to help it cut through a variety of metals and fiberglass. It is compact and lightweight, has a powerful 6amp motor with overload protection for smooth operation and longevity, features easy access for brush replacement, and comes with a sturdy high-impact box. Along with the saw and box, three cutting blades, a wrench, and a wrench holder are standard.

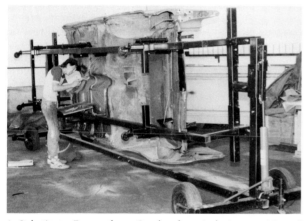

A Substitute Frame from Steelcrafters is being positioned under a 1957 Chevy body in one photo and is shown supporting that car body on a Mobile Lift in the other. This substitute frame incorporates eight pieces that adjust to accommodate and mount to almost any car body. Subframes offer plenty of reinforcement for weakened bodies and those which require extensive cutting and new panel installations, especially when used in combination with the Mobile Lift.

American Tool Companies

VISE-GRIP Locking C-Clamps come standard with swivel pads, making them perfect for securing items with awkwardly angled surfaces. These units work very well for supporting welding work, like the installation of brackets, panels, and other autobody attributes. Locking C-Clamps are offered in different sizes to accommodate the versatile needs of auto restorers and repair people. Each tool is adjustable in both jaw opening and tension strength. To release grips, simply depress the lever on the lower handle while holding the tool steady with your other hand on the upper handle.

TiP Sandblast Equipment

TiP Sandblast Equipment recognizes the needs of conscientious auto restorers who must remove years of accumulated rust and scale from neglected body panels while strongly wanting to preserve indicative stamping codes and other factory original indented markings. Even though this company manufactures sandblasting units for a wide range of uses, it caters to auto restorers with a long list of applicable equipment. Along with siphon and pressure sandblasters, the TiP Sandblast Equipment catalog lists a multitude of tool and equipment products, from pressure washers and high-volume, low-pressure (HVLP) painting systems to sandblast cabinets and buffing supplies, all designed with professional and do-it-yourself auto restorers and repair people in mind.

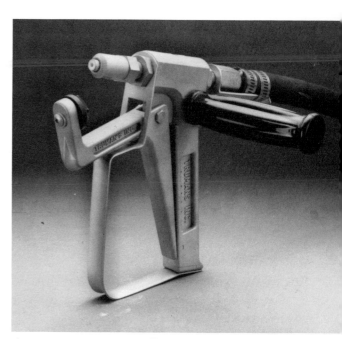

The TiP 99-S Pressure Sandblaster and accompanying 38 Special Trigger Operated Pressure Valve work hand in hand to meet auto restoration needs. This sandblasting unit is designed especially for the removal of rust, paint, and scale. The unit's tank measures 10in in diameter and is 25in tall. Combined with easy-handling wheels, it reaches an overall height of 35in. A total of 80lb to 90lb of sand can be poured into the sandblaster, which will offer about 20 minutes' blasting time. The trigger-operated pressure valve is great for detail work and fitting into extra-tight spaces. It uses abrasive resistant materials to stop sand flow and airflow instantly when its handle is released. The unit complies with Occupational Safety and Health Administration (OSHA) standards as a deadman shutoff valve and works exceptionally well with a 5hp or less powerful air supply. For intermittent use with small nozzles, plan to supply the unit with 7cfm at 80psi; a 3hp to 5hp air compressor is recommended. Standard equipment with the sandblaster includes a hood, a disposable dust mask, three nozzles, the 38 Special Trigger gun, an air-in valve, a mixing valve with a quick-clean-out feature, a choke valve, a pressure gauge, and 10ft of extra—heavy-duty sandblasting hose equipped with case-hardened fittings.

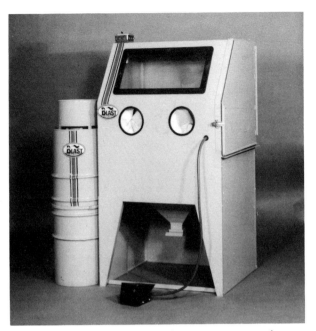

The Model 950 Glass Bead Cabinet is just one of many siphon-operated sandblasting cabinets manufactured by TiP. It is designed to remove paint, rust, and scale while continuously recycling abrasive. A foot pedal activates the nozzle flow. Abrasive drops down through a funnel for use again and again while a powerful vacuum removes dust that was created during the sandblasting process. A single switch operates both a floodlight and the vacuum. The cabinet is made with 20-gauge metal throughout and equipped with an 11-gauge steel door, angle iron framework, and an expanded metal screen capable of holding up to 200lb. The C-25 Power Gun has a case-hardened insert to provide it with a long working life, and its nozzle and air jets are available in three sizes. For continual and rapid production, a minimum 5hp air compressor is recommended. Standard accessories include an adjustable 150watt floodlight, tempered glass lens with inner lens protector, continual recycling system, full-size side loading door made of 11-gauge steel, C-25-M Power Gun, foot pedal, 6ft vacuum hose, central vacuum system with 110volt motor, and 25lb of abrasive. The unit requires 10cfm to 15cfm at 80psi, 7cfm with the small-nozzle and air jet setup.

The Eastwood Company

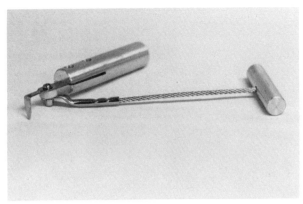

Newer vehicle windshields are glued into position with tough sealers. This seal has to be cut in order to remove broken windshield units. Some tools require two people for their operation. The Eastwood WINDSHIELD REMOVAL TOOL, however, is easily handled by just one person. The knife blade is angled to get up and under windshields while allowing plenty of room for users' hands. It is made of rugged metal, and the Super Blade will outlast standard replacement blades ten to one. Once the blade is placed in position under a windshield, the operator pulls on the cable handle while guiding the tool by its attached handle. Use caution during windshield cutting operations, and wear eye protection to guard eyes against glass fragments that could fly up, especially near broken glass sections.

The DOOR PANEL REMOVER from Eastwood was originally designed for use in aircraft upholstery shops and does an excellent job of gently loosening interior door panels from their clips. The poly wedge lifts panels smoothly, and the lightweight aluminum handle allows for excellent leverage in tight working spaces. Using a wide-bladed screwdriver or putty knife to remove panels could easily result in cuts, tears, or other damage. Before using this tool to pry loose the door panels, be certain armrests, window cranks, and door handles have been removed. Also make sure the panels on your car or truck are attached to the doors with push-on pins, not screws.

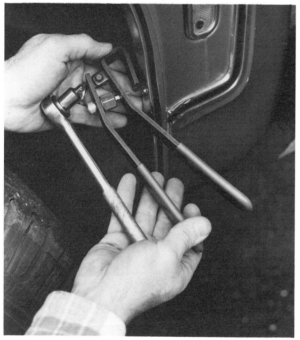

Active auto restorers and do-it-yourself enthusiasts will appreciate this tool when it comes time to remove heavily corroded trim screws from wheelwell moldings. The TRIM SCREW TOOL from Eastwood is worth its weight in gold when trying to fit a small Phillips-head screwdriver into trim screws and then amass enough leverage in awkward positions to loosen screws without rounding out their heads. Here, the hooklike grip fits around the back of the fender lips, and the plierslike handles force the Phillips-head bit into position once it is centered on a screw. While squeezing the handles to put lots of pressure directly on top of the screw head, the operator uses a $\frac{1}{4}$in ratchet or $\frac{5}{8}$in open-end wrench to turn the bit and loosen the screw.

Every automobile restoration project will result in the dismantling of many different parts, assemblies, and components. In most cases, many of these parts will remain idle for long periods of time before being put back on their host vehicle. This is why parts storage is a primary concern for all serious restorers. To help maintain an organized system for parts storage, consider using PARTS TAGS from Eastwood. They are equipped with handy metal ties and offer plenty of room for writing parts identifications and other pertinent notes with regard to special installation sequences or techniques. The tags are made of metal and designed to be written on with a ball-point pen. This way, if ink should fade, the metal tag will still remain embossed with the information written on it. The tags are waterproof and resistant to most garage chemicals. They come fifty to a package.

The kind of abrasive medium used and the pressure at which this material is applied combine to determine the amount of sandblasting force parts are subjected to. Heavy frame members and suspension parts may require a coarse abrasive and high air pressure application for the complete removal of all paint, rust, and scale deposits. Using that same medium and air pressure combination on a lighter-weight auto assembly, however, could result in catastrophic damage. Thin metal panels and other similar components require a less abrasive medium and lower–air pressure applications. These more delicate items cannot withstand heavy sandblasting and will likely warp, become heavily pitted, or even disintegrate if excessively sandblasted. To accommodate restorers, various abrasive medium products are available, like glass beads, aluminum oxide (shown here), and silicon carbide. Each has its own function range and purpose as determined by its coarseness in conjunction with the sandblaster tip size and air pressure settings.

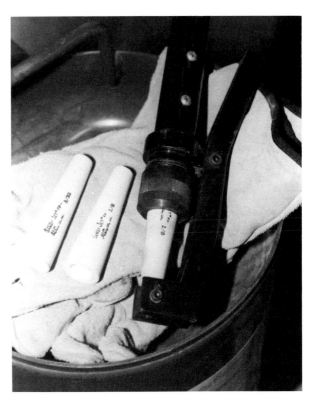

Sandblasting equipment plays a vital role in just about every major automobile restoration. The Model 110 Pressure Blaster comes equipped with a tank certified by the American Society of Mechanical Engineers (ASME), a spring-loaded on-off deadman valve, an easy-set mixing valve, a top-mounted gauge, a recessed tank top to make filling easy, a blast hood, three $^1/_8$in and one $^3/_{32}$in nozzles, and more. It is ideal for large and small jobs, like working on these seat brackets out of Mycon's 1948 Chevrolet. Pressure sandblasters are faster, use less air, and go through smaller amounts of abrasive medium than siphon units because the medium is forced out under pressure. Under normal working conditions with a $^1/_8$in nozzle, this unit can sandblast for 35 to 45 minutes before refills. Nozzles are easy to install and available in $^3/_{32}$in, $^1/_8$in, $^5/_{32}$in, $^3/_{16}$in, $^1/_4$in, and $^5/_{16}$in sizes. The $^3/_{32}$in and $^1/_8$in nozzles that come with this unit require a 2hp to 5hp air compressor, whereas the larger sizes need to be supplied by a 10hp to 40hp compressor. Charts are available to show which medium, nozzle, and air pressure combinations are most appropriate for the sandblasting you have planned.

Although sandblasting is a fast and efficient method of removing paint, rust, and scale from auto parts, it is a dusty and messy process. It is virtually impossible to escape the mess when working on large frames and suspensions, but sandblasting cabinets can make the task clean and easy when working on smaller auto parts and accessories. The Bench Blaster Sandblast Cabinet Kit from Eastwood is ideal for restorers with limited shop space and budgets. The unit is designed to rest on top of a workbench, which, in turn, makes room for storage areas underneath. It is shipped as a kit and an average assembly takes just 1 hour. The window is made of tempered glass and measures 24in by 12in. The full-size door is 22in by 22in, large enough for a variety of car parts. The Bench Blaster requires an air supply of 7cfm at 80psi to 100psi.

Solid sanding rolls are sometimes too rigid for the complete sanding of odd-shaped parts. To help with parts in need of more thorough sanding, try using the Sandboss, an inflatable rubber sanding roll shaped like a drum. Inflated sanding rolls offer wide cushioned work surfaces. They are available in three sizes: 1³/₄in diameter by 2in, 2¹/₂in diameter by 3¹/₄in, and 3¹/₂in diameter by 5¹/₄in. They all mount with a ¹/₄in shaft and can be used with electric drills, flexible grinding shafts, and drill presses. Sanding belts of assorted grits are also available in all three sizes. Inflation of each Sandboss is made through a regular tirelike air stem located at the bottom of the unit.

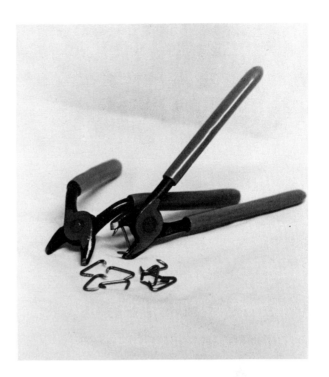

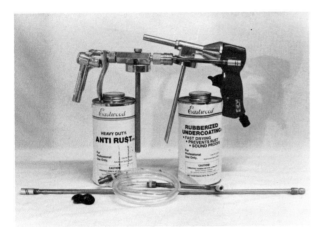

After the completion of each automotive repair and rejuvenation project, restorers concentrate on the application of rustproofing protection to all vulnerable body areas. Sometimes, this effort requires special rustproofing tools that are able to gain access into otherwise hidden body areas. Rustproofing accessibility is a major concern on automobiles that have not been completely dismantled for restoration. *Rustproofing* tools, consist of a spray nozzle, left, access wands, and an assortment of wand tips all designed for the application of brown spray-on films of rustproofing products, not to be confused with undercoating. Wands vary in length in order to reach into specific body cavities with the most convenience; they come long for entry into quarter panels and doors, short for rockers and fenders, and flexible for engine compartments and other areas. Plastic plugs are used to cover up holes that were drilled in door frames and rocker panels for access. Tips are individually machined to allow for directional spray variations. A back-angle spray tip has slots cut at an angle to allow rustproofing material to be sprayed back under a wand, such as below and up to access holes. The 90-degree tip covers everything at that angle, and the full-open nozzle will spray rustproofing material straight ahead. *Undercoating* materials generally produce layers of thick black film on auto underbody areas. More of a sound deadener and cushion against rocks and pebbles thrown up by tires, these materials are applied through a special gun, right. Although undercoating products may not offer actual rustproofing service, they will protect coats of rustproofing materials from exposure to and impact with harsh road debris.

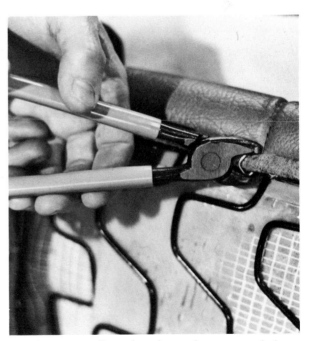

Hog rings are small metal staples used to secure upholstery fabric to seat frames. They are shaped in such a way that Hog Ring Pliers can easily maintain a grip on them while they are maneuvered into position. A simple squeeze of the pliers causes the rings to close so completely that their ends overlap. Grooves on the jaws of Hog Ring Pliers help the tools to hold rings steady at any angle. Along with straight Hog Ring Pliers, a bent model is available. The angled feature of these tools makes it easier for them to access some seat frame sections placed in otherwise-awkward-to-reach work areas. To assist work operations, the straight pliers are spring-loaded to stay closed, whereas the bent ones are spring-loaded to stay open.

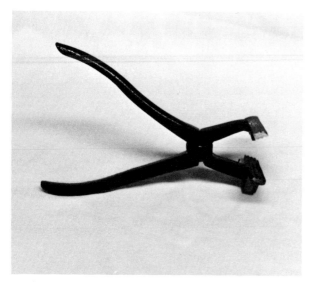

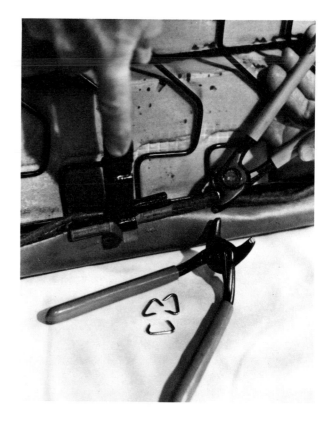

It is difficult stretching upholstery tight with just bare hands. That's why those in the professional auto upholstery business use tools like the Stretching Pliers. Gripped to the edge of a fabric section, this tool will stretch and hold material while Hog Ring Pliers are used to install hog rings. Ribbed jaws help this tool maintain its grip, and their 3½in width offers uniform pulling power. Built with a hammer jaw, this tool can be used as a lever to meet strong pull needs and as a hammer for tacks if necessary. The tool is made of forged steel and has an overall length of 8¾in.

Automobile restoration is not simply limited to bodywork and paint work. Interior upholstery needs must be met, too. Having the right tools on hand will almost always make jobs progress more smoothly and result in a nicer finish. The Auto Trimmer Knife from Eastwood is designed with a hook end that can slip into existing seams and cut old upholstery in such a way that restorers and upholsterers can use that material as a pattern for new fabric installations. The tool is made of tough cutlery steel and is rugged enough to be used for cutting carpet, vinyl, leather, plastic, and rubber. Be sure to keep the blade honed to a sharp edge for the most precise ease of cutting and crisp fabric edges.

Upholstery seams are easy to repair with the Automatic Awl from Eastwood. It can be used on seats, carpets, convertible tops, car covers, and other fabric accessories. Easy-to-read instructions quickly teach users how to make strong lock stitches. The top unscrews to open up a convenient storage place for needles and a handy screwdriver-wrench. A spool of waxed thread comes with the tool, and it is easy to remove and replace with other spools of thread in the colors needed for various projects. Spare needles in straight or curved designs are available, as are spools of brown or black thread.

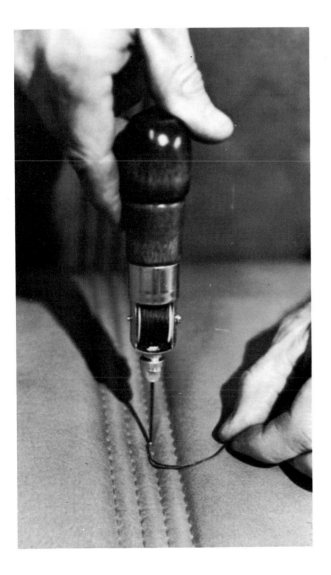

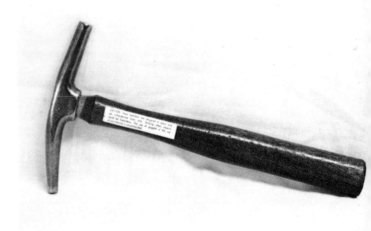

Some automobile models, especially the older ones, have seats mounted on pieces of wood instead of metal frames. For those, hog rings and Hog Ring Pliers are mostly useless; seat material is attached to the wood bases with tacks. The best way to drive these tacks is with the Magnetic Trim Tack Hammer. In addition to its handy size and light weight (only 7 ounces), this tool features a solid bronze head with a permanent alnico tip on one end. This magnetic steel tip is used to hold onto tack heads so that they can be driven with just one swing of the hammer. In other words, you will not have to hold tacks carefully with a thumb and finger from one hand while trying to smack just a tack head with the hammer in your other hand. This tool can help save on sore thumbs and fingers, as well as allow your free hand to hold fabrics taut as they are tacked in place.

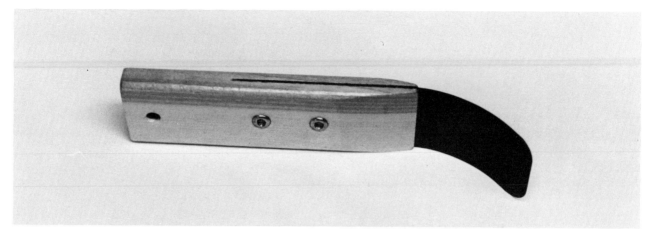

Slipping headliner material edges into their appropriate grooves and holders is sometimes difficult without the help of the Headliner Tucking Tool from Eastwood. This unit's rounded edges will not cut or damage material, and its angled blade works very well for reaching into corners.

Along with headliners, you could also use it for tucking other upholstery materials into trim. The tool is much safer and more efficient than putty knives and other flat tools with sharp corners.

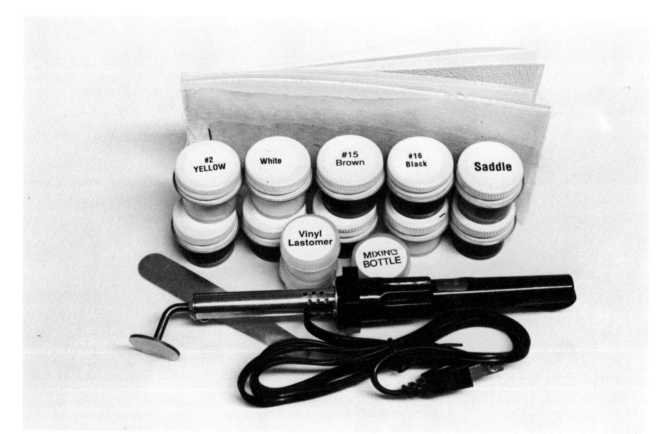

Auto restorations sometimes involve vinyl accessory repair. In some cases, just a tiny blemish is the only problem with a vinyl piece. In lieu of purchasing an expensive complete replacement for slightly marred items, consider repairing them with Eastwood's Vinyl Repair Kit. The kit's liquid compounds become flexible vinyl after they are properly applied and heat cured. Step-by-step instructions guide users through a process that eventually backs vinyl damage with a fabric insert, covers blemishes or tears with a mixture that chemically bonds to all surrounding areas, and makes the bonding mixture appear as though repairs were never made by way of graining materials that emboss duplicates of original vinyl finishes. This kit contains enough supplies for dozens of repairs. Along with ten different compound colors that can be intermixed, according to the enclosed color chart, to match vinyl colors scheduled for repair, the kit also includes graining sheets, a spatula, and the Micro Disc heating tool.

Chapter 5

Metal Fabrication Tools

Avid and serious do-it-yourself automobile enthusiasts who actively restore, modify, or customize automobiles are familiar with the special needs that relate to metal fabrication. Often, sheet metal replacement parts are no longer available for restoration vehicles, and custom-fit modifications simply require special-made sheet metal sections. To make it easier to fabricate metal stock into viable pieces of tight-fitting sheet metal, a variety of tools, equipment, and unique machinery are available.

It takes practice working with tools and equipment to learn how to fabricate a metal part correctly on the first try. Likewise, the ability to accurately correct mistakes made on original bends, cuts, or welds separates experienced professionals from novices. As you become more familiar with the implements you will use to make custom panels and other parts, your level of expertise will rise. No expert metal fabricator was simply born with talents that never needed

nurturing or instruction. So-called natural talents were honed to perfection through years of practicing, studying how other jobs were completed, and watching other, more experienced artisans.

Using the right tools according to operator instructions, you can bend, cut, shape, and weld various sizes of metal into almost any shape. Metal stock is purchased through companies that deal in the products found in the Yellow Pages under the heading for steel distributors and warehouses.

Tools that cut, bend, shape, and weld metal can also cut, crush, or burn your fingers, hands, face, and any other part of your body. This is why strict personal safeguards are always instituted at steel plants and metal fabrication shops. Any type of flame-producing tool operation requires eye and hand protection; this includes torch cutting, plasma cutting, and all welding. Hot metal sparks do not cool down quickly. Once they land on your hand, wrist, or arm, they will continue to burn your skin a lot longer than is tolerable. The extremely bright light emitted from welding operations can permanently injure eyes with

Foreign Car Specialties

This English Wheeling Machine model was inspired by the traditional lines and stoutness of the early-twentieth-century English Wheels. The unit incorporates a heavy-duty cast-iron frame that is intended to eliminate any problems associated with frame flexing. Great attention to detail was put into the choice of a dropforged upper wheel and easily adjusted lower wheel with quick-release capability. Wheeling machines are used to produce compound curves from flat sheet metal stock. Metal is inserted between the upper wheel and the adjustable lower wheel. Tension is adjusted on the lower wheel to squeeze just the right amount of curve into the panels. Operators push and pull the panels back and forth, causing the metal slowly to develop a slight curve. Continued rolling and adjustment will eventually turn out a product *wheeled* to the shape desired. On the base of the lower wheel, between upright frame members, are three additional small wheels. These are used as needed to acquire various curves and contours.

brief periods of exposure. Therefore, always plan to wear appropriate shaded welding helmets, heavy-duty leather gloves with long gauntlets, a filter mask, and a leather apron that will repel the effects of hot metal sparks.

Right Angle Tool Company

The Right Angle Tool Company manufactures replacement parts, as well as equipment and tools used for turning flat stocks of metal into viable pieces. The company prides itself on offering quality tools at competitive prices. Professional and do-it-yourself autobody repair people, restorers, and customizers in need of products that can turn out precision replacement parts or modifications should consider these items as affordable workshop attributes. The list of metal fabrication tools available from the Right Angle Tool Company includes shrinkers-stretchers, shears, brakes, slip rolls, notchers, rotary machines, and more.

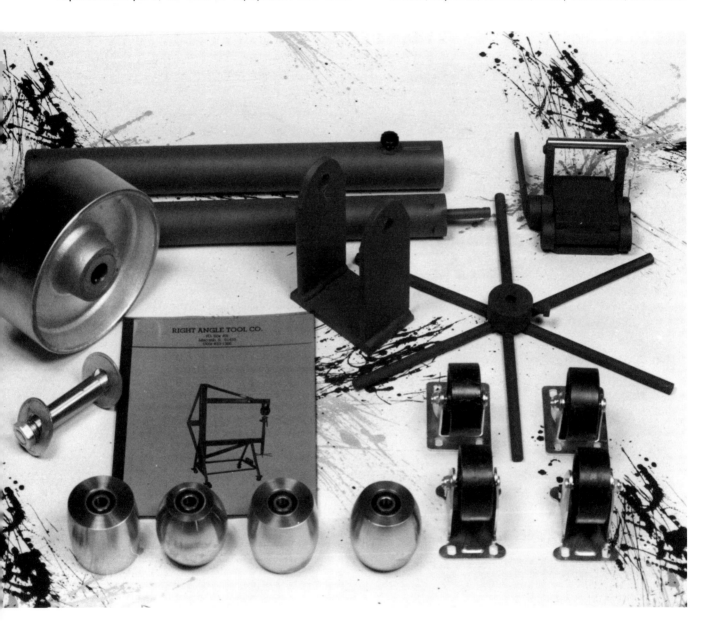

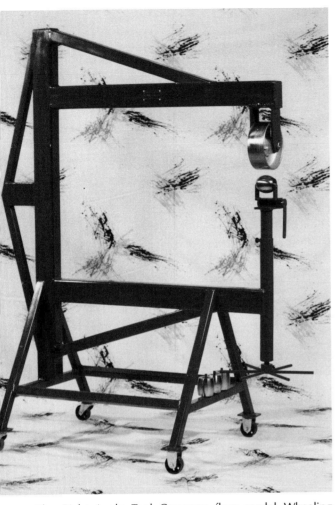

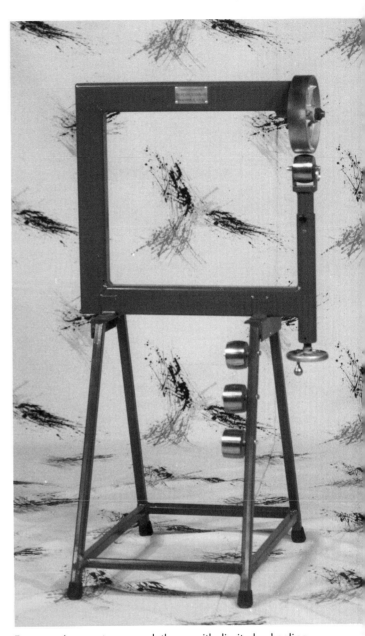

The Right Angle Tool Company floor model Wheeling Machine has a 44in throat depth, a quick-release cam, and four anvil wheels and is strong enough to accommodate 18-gauge steel or $\frac{1}{8}$in aluminum. The unit is designed for forming compound curves in sheet metal to reproduce body panels. Stock is inserted between the rollers, and pressure is applied by turning the lower adjuster. Rolling metal back and forth between the rollers will cause the metal to take the shape of the curved lower roller. Basically, the process is a controlled stretching of metal that results in a smooth surface finish. With just a little practice, users generally develop a natural rhythm that finds them overlapping each pass for precise curves. This process is just slow enough that conscientious operators seldom get too far ahead of their work and create excessive curves. Along with the floor model, Right Angle offers the convenient and more affordable U-Weld Kit. This kit contains all the parts and pieces needed to produce the floor model except for the steel frame tubing, which is purchased and welded together separately by customers. The kit includes step-by-step instructions.

For part-time restorers and those with limited wheeling needs, the handy Bench Model wheeling machine may be an appropriate resource. It is an affordable model that many do-it-yourselfers might consider an entry-level machine used to fabricate small auto component items. It could also serve as an ideal wheeling machine for those who need an introduction into the craft without the larger tool expenditure. This unit has a 22in throat, which makes it capable of working to the center of body panels up to 44in wide. It can be permanently mounted to a workbench, used as a portable unit by being clamped in a vise, or placed on the optional stand. Users can roll up to 20-gauge mild steel with excellent results.

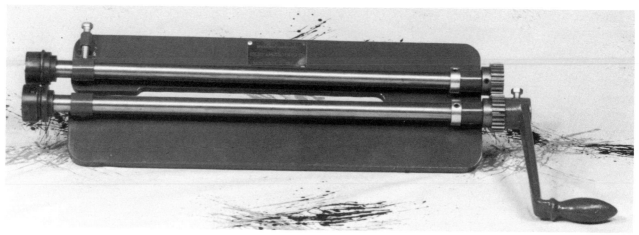

The Bead Roller from Right Angle Tool Company is used to "roll in" strengthening beads on sheet metal panels. Custom-made die sets are available that will reproduce the body moldings featured on the original panels of older automobile makes and models. This machine can also roll in wire beading in fender edges, overlap seams for flush welding, fold over edges on curved panels, shear, and a lot more. This 20in-throat model is made of strong ⅝in steel plate and comes with a ¼in die set.

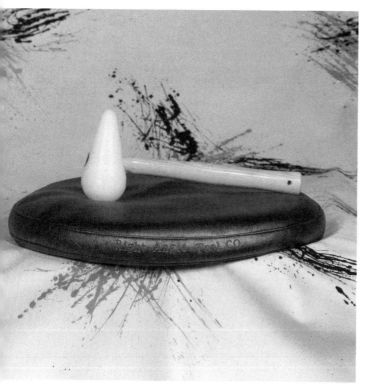

Anyone who shapes sheet metal should have the Panel Beater Bag. This 18in round bag is double stitched and can be filled with sand or lead shot. Optional mallets are used to pound on sheet metal to form them into desired curves. Many times, users are able to rough out initial panel curves on this bag and then finish those forms to smooth perfection on a wheeling machine. In addition, the Panel Beater Bag can be used during repair work to pound out small dings and imperfections. The filler material inside this bag will support sheet metal and yet give just enough under mallet blows to allow metal to stretch into shape.

The Motorized Flame Cutter from Right Angle Tool Company is used to make brackets or copy any shape when utilized with a pattern. It is a full production flame cutter that features a rheostat-driven motor and the Victor Machine Torch. Metal patterns are traced with a magnetic device, and a straight bar is used for general straight cutting. This machine offers incredibly smooth cuts that can be reproduced over and over again with exact precision. For automobile rebuilders faced with a great quantity of metal fabrication requirements, especially when numerous identical parts or panels that can be patterned are needed, this tool could pay for itself in short order.

Smithy Company

Smithy Company offers milling, turning, and drilling tools and equipment for professional and do-it-yourself metal fabricators. Users have relied on Smithy for operations in light industry, auto restoration, mechanical work, and general auto repair. The company's toll-free telephone number also serves as a hot line that customers are invited to use when needing support or technical assistance with fabrication or repair projects.

The Smithy AT-300 Power Feed combination lathe, mill, and drill offers most of the capabilities and features of full-sized machinery but only takes up the space of an ordinary mechanic's tool chest. It uses a 110volt electrical service and standard tools. Tapers on the headstock, milling head, and tailstock are all industry standard Morse tapers. Manufactured to light industrial standards, this unit is precision built with average tolerances within 0.001in to 0.002in. A complete line of optional accessory tools includes items like shaped cutters, rotary tables, adjustable vises, drill chucks, and more. Setup preparations must be made before the delivery of a Smithy because the machine, tools, and shipping crate together weigh over 500lb. Instructions for uncrating and setting up the tool are mailed to customers some time before delivery to help them prepare for those operations. The lathe can be used to turn materials as hard as high-carbon steel or as soft as wood. It can make compound angles and cut SAE or metric threads in standard sizes. The lathe-boring feature is used to mill or bore large-diameter holes or enlarge the cylinders on small engine blocks. The drill press and mill can be used interchangeably on the same project without having to reset work.

Black and Decker

Perfectly straight cuts are easy to make on piping up to 4in in diameter and bar stock as thick as 2½in with the Heavy Duty 14in Chop Saw from Black and Decker. Its powerful 13amp motor moves the blade at a speed of up to 3800rpm and can be set up to operate on AC or a generator's DC power supply. The tool weighs 36lb and comes with a 14in blade and wrench. For quick, precise cuts on all kinds of metal stock, consider this chop saw a worthwhile investment. It works well for a wide range of duties, from cutting exhaust pipe and bracket material to slicing rod stock and square tubing.

American Tool Companies

The PROSNIP Tinner Snips are heavy-duty. They can easily and cleanly cut through sheet metal, metal strapping, plastic, rubber, canvas, cardboard, screening, carpet, vinyl, and a lot more. The steel blades are forged, not stamped. Long handles with soft vinyl covers assist users with leverage and comfort, and the serrated blades give this tool extra gripping strength. This item is used for all kinds of auto restoration and repair needs, from cutting away damaged sections to creating patch panel pieces.

VISE-GRIP Locking Bar Clamps are familiar tools found in just about every autobody and restoration shop. They come in both 10in and 18in bar lengths. They are commonly used for holding metal pieces together for welding, for stabilizing auto parts as sections are dismantled or put together, as clamps for parts grinding or polishing endeavors, and for a great many more tasks. The locking feature is adjusted by pushing the free end close to the piece being worked on while the operating jaw is open. Twisting a knurled screw at the base of a handle will allow the locking jaw to come closer or move farther away from a piece being held. Once the jaw is set to its grip position, the handles are squeezed together to lock parts in place, just as a vise is locked in place. The tool is released by depressing a small lever on the other handle.

The 5-Piece VISE-GRIP Welding Tool Set includes two 11in locking C-clamps, two 6in locking C-clamps, and a 10in straight-jaw locking pliers tool; the long-flanged Welding Clamp is sold separately. For two pieces of metal to be welded together, they must be held securely in position. VISE-GRIP tools are perfect implements for such purposes. They are easy to handle, set up, and secure. Various jaw sizes nicely accommodate different material widths and shapes. Their grip, when adjusted tightly, will not let go until the release lever is depressed. Most avid and professional restorers, metal fabricators, and autobody technicians have numerous VISE-GRIP clamping tools at their disposal because often they require up to a dozen individual clamps to secure large body panels or metal stock sections. The Welding Clamp is designed with wide-fingered flat flanges on the bottom and angled flanges on the top. This tool design is perfect for reaching over lips, bent metal edges, and obstructions. It is also great for holding the edges of two separate metal pieces together for perfect seam or butt welding.

Plano Molding Company

The Plano Molding Company manufactures and distributes a wide range of tough plastic toolboxes, storage boxes, and handy tray units for a variety of uses and applications. Rugged, lightweight, and easy-to-clean plastic boxes and organizers have qualities that are tough for some metal counterparts to match. Plastic does not weigh as much as metal; its corners and edges are not sharp; it won't rust, chip, dent, peel, or rattle; and when combined with sturdy, solid brass latch mechanisms, it will secure your tools, fasteners, and other goodies for a long time. In fact, Plano backs each molded plastic toolbox and organizer with a lifetime guarantee.

Plano's red, gray, and black #872 Two Drawer System toolbox makes an ideal storage and carrying unit for a host of VISE-GRIP clamps, an HTP America Flanger and Belt Sander, an Eastwood Nibbler, and a lot more welding hand tools. It is handy to have all related working tools grouped together in one convenient toolbox so that they can all be on a job site at the same time. Many meticulous auto enthusiasts prefer to have separate smaller toolboxes set aside for special work tools instead of having those items strewn about in large tool chests. This way, they can retrieve one or two boxes and have all working implements immediately at their side, as opposed to making a number of trips back to assorted tool chest drawers.

Harbor Freight Tools

The 18in Metal Bending Brake is used to bend sheet metal stock and other lighter-gauge pieces into straight angles of varying degrees. The tool is secured to a workbench with clamps—in this case, VISE-GRIP C-clamp tools. A piece of metal is laid on top of the tool with the impending bend positioned on top of the hinged joint. A piece of flat stock (brake) is then clamped on top of the work piece—here, using standard C-clamps. Handles are provided to help users lift a hinged bar and move it forward. That pressure causes the work piece to bend at the hinge and along the edge of the brake. Metal pieces can be bent up to 90 degrees. The tool can also be permanently mounted to workbenches by securing heavy-duty screws through holes placed on the base.

HTP America

HTP America has spent considerable time designing and manufacturing its MIG welders and plasma cutters to suit the needs of almost all auto restorers, metal fabricators, and autobody specialists. The company has also produced a videotape that explains exactly how its products are put together, adjusted, and used. The tape covers everything from installing wire reels and dismantling and assembling welder handles to operating plasma cutters properly and maintaining the tips of tools. Should you buy an HTP America product, you are urged also to acquire the videotape.

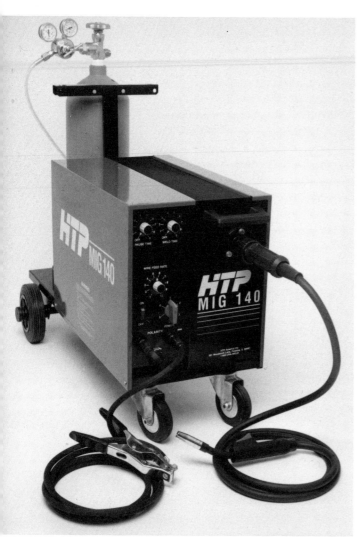

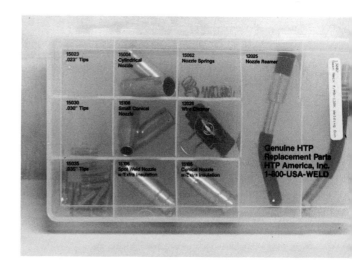

The HTP MIG Consumable Kit is an optional accessory that should be part of your welder equipment. It includes a nozzle reamer, a swan neck, six 0.023in tips, six 0.03in tips, three 0.035in tips, two conical nozzles, two small conical nozzles, two cylindrical nozzles, two spot weld nozzles, a wire cleaner, and five nozzle springs. This is a complete replacement parts kit that includes a sectioned container, which is labeled for easy reference. Welding parts do wear out after a while, and you will be ready to replace them with this kit. The training video and operating instructions cover all installation and use procedures.

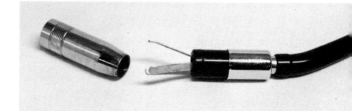

The HTP Nozzle Reamer is used to scrape away slag and other debris spattered up by normal welding processes to keep nozzles from clogging with this debris. Using the Nozzle Reamer to remove build-up keeps nozzle openings clear enough for the passage of welding wire and gas. The tool's fingers are spring loaded to expand as they exit the tool. The reamer's finger end is placed against a nozzle opening with the fingers fully retracted. Then, the reamer handle is pushed forward to force the fingers inside the nozzle opening. In this position, the tool is rotated so that the fingers can scrape the nozzle walls and break away debris.

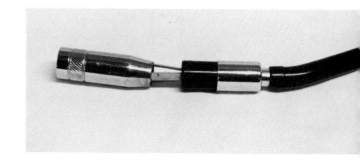

MIG welding equipment has become as common to auto-body metal fabrication and repair as hammers and dollies. Instead of using wire feed rolls that include flux, MIG welders rely on a gas mixture to make the immediate welding atmosphere inert and allow the use of plain wire rolls for welding. This makes for much cleaner welds because no flux material is left behind that needs to be chipped and wire-brushed off. One ideal feature of both the HTP MIG 110 and MIG 140 welders is that they operate off of a 110volt electrical service; a separate 220volt outlet need not be wired in, although you should provide a 30amp circuit breaker for operations that will utilize the tools' full capacity. Along with many outstanding features, these welders include copper windings in both the transformer and coil; a main relay mechanism to keep welding wire "off" until the gun trigger is depressed; continuous-stitch, spot, and seam welding adjustments; and the capability to braze steel and weld aluminum, steel, stainless steel, and cast iron. The drive mechanism is all-steel construction with a single-lever pressure release mechanism and unique U-shaped grooves for greater wire contact than with traditional V-shaped groove designs. The compact design, sturdy frame, and heavy-duty wheels of these units make them easy to move and maneuver. The MIG 110 can weld materials to a maximum of $^1/_8$in to $^3/_{16}$in thick, whereas the MIG 140 (shown here) can handle thicknesses up to $^3/_{16}$in to $1^2/_5$in.

Welding new autobody panel sections to old ones is not easy unless a flange is crimped along the edge of one unit so that the thin, straight edge of the other can slip up to and butt against it. This process provides a narrow strip of depressed sheet metal on one panel to lay behind the sheet metal edge of the other panel. Along with lending support to help clamps secure the pieces and providing for more rigid welds, it offers much better "lap" welding conditions, as opposed to just having two straight, thin edges next to each other, requiring a butt weld. The HTP Combination Punch and Flange Tool does an excellent job of pressing flanges. Long handles give users plenty of leverage and will flange metal to a width of $7/8$in width and an offset depth of $1/25$in. The tool's head can be loosened with the turn of a bolt to allow users to rotate the head to a hole punch mechanism. You have a choice of $3/16$in or IICAR-recommended $5/16$in holes. This feature is used when planning to make MIG plug welds on panels. The tool will punch or flange up to 20-gauge metal.

The HTP Nozzle Shield and Anti-Spatter Spray is applied to nozzles, tips, and swan necks to help prevent spatter build-up from sticking to their surfaces. It is not a silicone product, but, rather, a special antispatter formula. It is designed for use on all MIG welding guns, contact tips, and surfaces where spatter from welding is objectionable.

The ease and convenience of welding with the HTP MIG 140 are enhanced when welds are ground smooth with the HTP Belt Sander. The versatile corner end of this sander works very well for smoothing welds located in 90-degree corners. This pneumatic sander can be adjusted to a number of various angles, and replacement belts come in various grits.

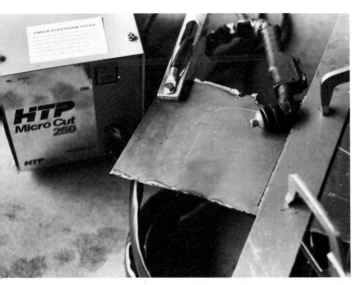

The HTP Micro Cut 250 Plasma Cutter is designed for professional bodyshops and serious do-it-yourselfers. It can cut through painted sheet metal with no distortion or paint damage more than $\frac{1}{16}$in away from cuts. The versatility of this tool enables it to cut through $\frac{1}{4}$in steel, stainless steel, or aluminum as if it were tinfoil. A 220volt outlet must be provided for this unit, as well as an air pressure source. This cutter includes features like three safety circuits and a 100 percent copper wound transformer and weighs only 60lb. The Micro Cut 250 will cut all conductive metals with low heat input and low distortion. The jagged open ends of this piece of metal stock were cut with a torch. Along the straight-edge guide held in place with VISE-GRIP clamps, though, the Micro Cut 250 was easily able to cut a straight, crisp line with no noticeable distortion. Operation is simple: Plug the unit into its 220volt power outlet, connect an air compressor hose to the unit, set the air pressure regulator at 80psi to 100psi, depress the gun trigger, and push down on the gun tip to activate the cutting arc. You must wear gloves and a welding hood with a dark lens.

Like MIG welders, plasma cutters also experience worn tips. As it does for its MIG welders, HTP also offers a complete replacement kit for plasma cutters, called the Micro Cut 250 Consumable Kit. You are encouraged to watch HTP's training video and read the owner's manual before connecting or attempting to use your Micro Cut 250. A lot of valuable setup and operational instructions are included in both resources. Haphazardly using this type of equipment without studying directions could result in wasted metal stock, damage to the machine, or personal injury.

The Eastwood Company

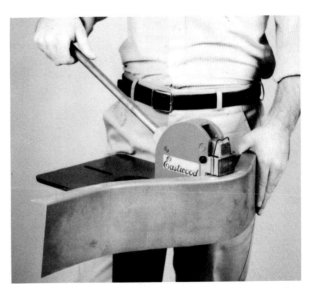

Eastwood's Compact Bender is used to fabricate steel into a variety of bends. Users can work with flat, square, or round solid stock in sizes ranging up to ⁵⁄₁₆in-by-2in strap and ⁵⁄₈in round or square solid bar stock. The bender must be securely bolted to the floor in order to remain steady while leverage is applied on it. The long handle shown resting vertically against the bender fits into the head piece and is secured with heavy-duty pins. When this handle is not in use, remove it so that it is out of the way. A series of round rollers are stored on pins welded to the tool's upright pedestal. Each has a specific purpose for obtaining certain bends of varying degrees, from crisp 90-degree angles to smooth round arcs. This tool comes with all the attachments needed to make a wide variety of brackets, U-shaped clamps, pinned holders, and more. The instruction manual is mandatory reading. Plan to keep it handy near the bender for frequent referral. The manual is definitive and will show you how to use this tool to all of its advantages.

The Shrinker/Stretcher tool is used to create smooth radius bends in metal without having to cut, hammer, or heat material. Bolted to your workbench or a sturdy pedestal, this unit can multiply your muscle power by forty-five, supplying plenty of pressure for the tool's hardened steel jaws. In these photos, a person is *shrinking* metal into a tight radius, left, and the tool is *stretching* metal, right. Once a 90-degree angled lip has been put on a piece of stock, which is generally done with a bending brake, either shrinker or stretcher jaws inserted into this tool will form the arcs needed to reproduce wheelwell flanges, compound doglegs, and even trunk corners. Curves as tight as a 3in radius are possible. The tool can shape mild steel up to 18 gauge, stainless steel up to 20 gauge, and aluminum up to 16 gauge. The parts displayed here were first bent in a brake before shrinking or stretching and are 18-gauge mild steel.

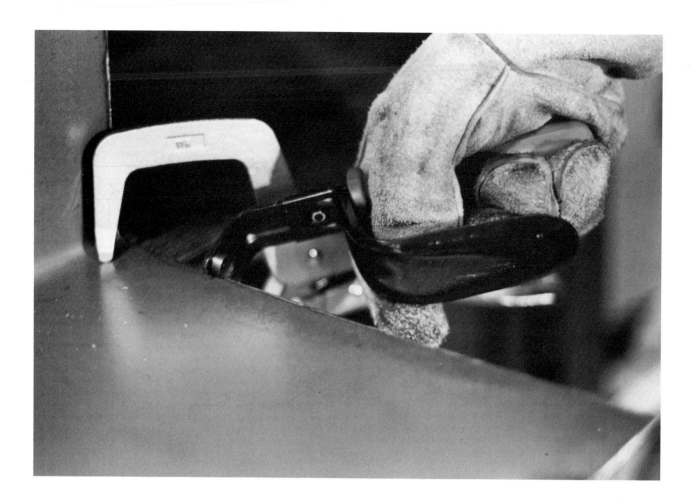

The Deburring Tool uses two extrahard and very sharp round blades to scrape rough burrs off the edges of sheet metal panels and plates from ¹/₃₂in to ¹/₂in thick. As the tool is pulled along the edge of the panel, burrs are shaved off from both sides. The adjustable round blades can be rotated periodically to ensure a long working life. This tool is not only good for metal fabrication work, it can be used to smooth rough edges on existing body panels, thus removing sharp hand- and arm-cutting hazards, to make working on panels safer. When working with metal tools like this, you should wear heavy-duty gloves just in case your hand or the tool slips off of work surfaces.

Welding two pieces of metal together at an angle is not always easy. The Magnetic Welding Jig can prove helpful, however. It has magnetic power on all of its sides to position metal pieces in a number of different angle positions, including 90, 75, 60, 45, and 30 degrees. It has over 12lb of holding strength and measures 4in by 2¹/₂in. More than one unit can be used together for holding larger items. In the position displayed here, tack welds are made to secure metal parts. Once tack welds are achieved, the unit can be removed for unobstructed welding. Drawings on the side of the tool indicate how perspective angles are laid out.

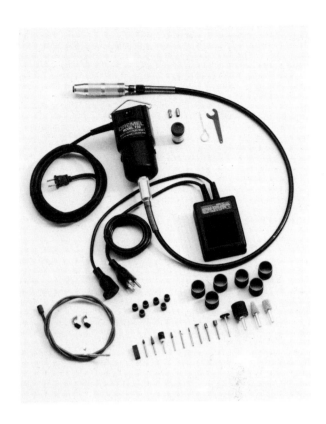

The Compact Bender operates on a simple leverage theory. Rollers, or a square- or triangular-shaped block, or both are used in various combinations and at strategic locations, enabling users to apply pressure on metal stock from a long bar. Holes located around the head piece and lever are used for positioning rollers and blocks in assorted patterns. Leverage forces metal to conform to the shape designed by roller and block positions. A "stop" pin that is included will cause the bar to cease bending at the same location each time. It is used for occasions when a number of identical parts need to be made and the lever has to stop at the same place each time in order to bend pieces identically with each motion. Rollers and blocks are held in position by sturdy pins, which are equipped with rugged handles for easy removal and insertion.

Dremel

The Dremel #7390 Heavy-Duty Flex-Shaft Kit can be used for all kinds of intricate auto restoration and small metal fabrication needs. Various tips are capable of grinding, cutting, and polishing metal parts. This hard-working tool can easily make the difference between a mediocre custom instrument panel or an outstanding one. Consider this tool for workbench tasks that involve setting gauges, toggle switches, grommets, and a host of other items on custom-made interior modifications. The varied capabilities of this high-speed (20,000rpm) tool are virtually limitless. It can even be put to work on engine heads for fine polishing. The motor has a built-in hanger, and the hand piece is made to grip comfortably. Variable speeds are regulated by a foot control. Accessory items available for Dremel tools include high-speed cutters, brushes, drum sanders, aluminum oxide stones, and tungsten carbide cutters.

Chapter 6

Autobody Repair Tools

The simple term autobody repair may conjure up myriad automotive projects to anyone deeply involved with the restoration or meticulous maintenance of any car or truck. For the most part, though, anything generally connected with the term *autobody* usually has something to do with the repair of sheet metal damage, like dings, dents, creases, and so on.

Pounding out dents on fenders, quarter panels, roofs, and doors requires some expertise and a lot of patience. The materials used for sheet metal car bodies in the 1950s and 1960s were a great deal thicker and heavier than the materials used for autobody panels on cars today and generally since the 1970s. Simply put, older and heavier panels were able to be repaired with heat and metal filler materials, whereas the newer paper-thin panels can only be flattened so far and must then be coated with plastic fillers.

Except for the fortunate autobody technicians who are employed by professional restoration shops that work mostly on older vehicles, many professional autobody technicians in the general field today see "old-fashioned" leading-in and soldering work as becoming a lost art. In fact, with labor fees and overhead costs skyrocketing everywhere, the autobody repair business has almost become a remove-and-replace operation. This is because in many cases it is less expensive in the long run to pay for new fenders and door skins than to pay the labor costs for flattening out, filling in, and sanding such easily replaceable parts.

For those who prefer to do their own bodywork, a great deal of money can be saved by spending time repairing panels and auto attributes instead of replacing them. The art of using hammers and dollies requires practice, and you are encouraged to read books about this operation and find an old door or fender to practice on.

You will need a variety of tools if you expect to complete autobody repair jobs in a professional and timely manner. Numerous tools and pieces of equipment are available, all of which require a thorough understanding of how they are designed to be operated and cared for. Take time to read instructions that accompany new tools and equipment. This will help you to use them confidently and safely. Be sure to wear face shields and gloves whenever called for and consider ear protection while operating loud power tools.

Snap-on Tools Corporation

Wheel alignment machines may not be on every do-it-yourselfers' list of desired shop equipment, but they could pay for themselves at busy repair and restoration shops or for those who conduct a lot of that kind of work on their own. The WA2000 Drive-on Alignment Ramp from Snap-on has a capacity of 8,000lb and can be used to perform two- and four-wheel alignments on cars and light trucks. Sturdy ramp-mounted front-wheel stops can be removed for cars or trucks with a low front end. This unit offers users a number of interesting features, all designed to make alignment work progress easier, more quickly, and more accurately.

Chief Automotive Systems

Chief Automotive Systems is in the business of making autobody collision repair a state-of-the-art operation. Development of frame-straightening machines and devices to make repair shops more versatile is a foremost consideration. To help technicians realize the full potential of Chief products, this company continues to provide training with every equipment placement.

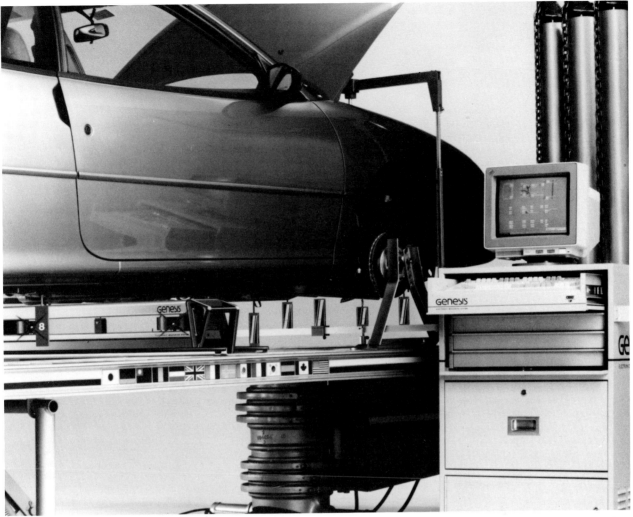

For straightening autobody frames and related components, Chief Automotive Systems has developed the Genesis Electronic Measuring System. This revolutionary system incorporates three advanced technologies for optimal accuracy and unparalleled productivity: the computer, the laser, and electronic components. The Genesis is claimed to be the fastest and most accurate measuring system ever developed. It can complete specification updates every few seconds and is designed to be left in place throughout entire repair processes; it does not have to be set up again after each pull or part replacement. The computerized system begins with a data base of the vehicle's specifications with graphic displays and control point specifics of the vehicle's structure. Its body scanner automatically reads all reference points simultaneously from strategically placed targets throughout the vehicle. These readings are then compared with published data and are displayed in color on the monitor screen. Basically, the Genesis is able to inform technicians exactly which parts are aligned and which ones are not. Then, efforts are undertaken to pull damaged sections back in place in accordance with data base information.

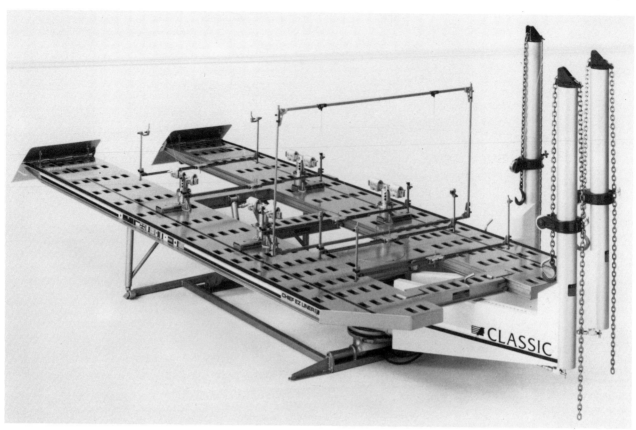

The Chief EZ Liner Classic offers a simultaneous multiple pulling method and 360-degree access. This unit can handle the frame- and body-straightening needs of a full range of unitized cars, conventional frame vehicles, vans, pickup trucks, and four-wheel drives. The Classic can perform a wide variety of complex pulls by means of a unique combination of infinitely adjustable rotating towers and portable rams. This unit can simultaneously make down-pulls, above-the-beltline pulls, and rocker panel side pulls using the Universal Anchoring System as clamps; with proper attachments, pulls can be multiplied from one or more towers or rams. The theory behind this special piece of equipment is that damage should be pulled out in exactly the reverse direction it was incurred. When a collision occurs, the damaging forces are transferred throughout an autobody structure at various angles that are unique in every case. The Classic permits all of those angles to be reversed precisely and simultaneously.

HTP America

The HTP Combination Punch and Flange Tool is used to create a lip along replacement sheet metal panels. This narrow projection can then slip under existing panel edges for support while its host piece can maintain a surface area at the same level as an existing sheet metal section. Flanging new patch panels is very important. Along with offering rigid support, flanges make welding a lot easier and more thorough by providing for a lap weld as opposed to a simple butt weld. The head of this tool can swivel so that a punch mechanism can be used. Holes are punched in sheet metal panels to accommodate plug welding techniques. Plug welds hold tight and do not require long periods of welding time for their completion. This is an advantage when welding on auto panels made of thin sheet metal, as extensive and prolonged welding will cause the metal to warp and distort.

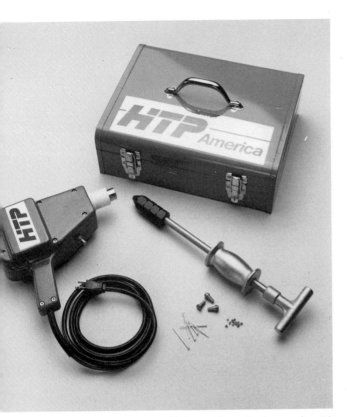

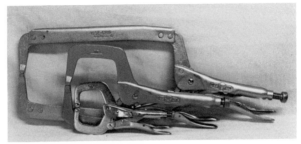

VISE-GRIP Clamps are mainstay tools in almost every body repair facility. They are perfect for holding sheet metal pieces together while fastening operations are underway. The long-reaching tools can span over uninvolved areas to connect where needed—a typical requirement for technicians working on odd-shaped panels. Once squarely and securely placed and clamped, these tools will hold tight during welding, grinding, and other metal operations.

Years ago, dents were pulled out of autobody panels with picks and hammers. In essence, a series of holes were drilled along the center of dent damage, and hooked T-handled picks were inserted into them. Technicians could grab hold of the picks and pull dents out, occasionally tapping on crowns with body hammers to reduce them. With the HTP Stud Setter, bodyworkers have no reason to drill holes in panels for picks. This tool welds short studs to damaged areas, and the slide hammer attaches over these studs and secures to them. Technicians use the slide hammer to pull out dents and also to apply outward pressure on dents while tapping crowns with a body hammer. Studs are easily clipped off with side-cutters and then ground smooth. The Stud Setter is also capable of installing trim rivets. Simply attach the trim rivet tip, place a rivet in its magnetic end, hold work up to its scribed line, and pull the trigger; an electrical charge does all the rest. Metal can be shrunk with clean electric heat from this gun, too. Once a spot is heated, tap it with a body hammer and cool it off with a sopping wet rag.

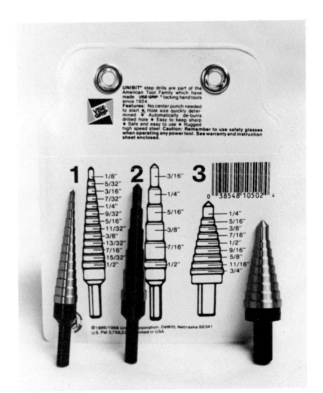

UNIBIT Step Drills use a unique single-flute design to drill perfectly round holes in any thin material with less effort than traditional twist drills. These drills incorporate cutting steps of progressively larger diameters, allowing users to drill up to thirteen different hole sizes with a single bit. Self-starting nonskid tips start each hole quickly, eliminating the need to center punch, even on curved surfaces. The Step Drills shown here are capable of drilling holes from $1/8$in to a full $3/4$in. Optional models can drill holes as big as $1\,3/8$in.

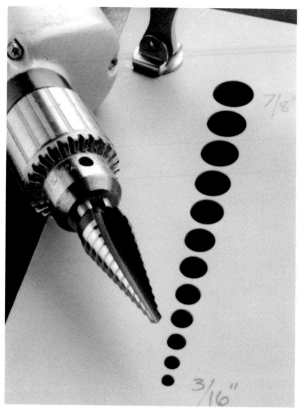

These tools are handy and convenient. In lieu of your searching for specific sizes of twist drill bits, one or the other of these three could easily accommodate most of your autobody repair needs.

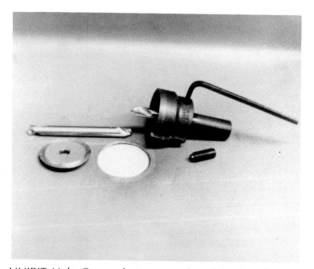

UNIBIT Carbide Hole Cutters feature a specially designed carbide insert that ensures cutting edge longevity and self-ejects slugs upon completion of hole drilling. A 135-degree pilot drill with a split tip and double end helps eliminate the need for center punching and prevents vibration chatter in soft materials. These tools work with great speed in sheet metal, brass, copper, aluminum, stainless steel, fiberglass, and other materials. Users will like the way they cut perfectly round holes with no scuffing or damage to surrounding areas. The automotive kit includes 3/4in, 7/8in, 1in, 1 1/8in, 1 1/4in, and 1 1/2in sizes, along with a small kit that holds two spare pilot bits, a hex key wrench, and a spare setscrew.

UNIBIT Hole Cutters feature a replaceable pilot drill bit. These bits are double ended, which means they should give you twice the working life of a single-tipped unit. A small setscrew holds pilot bits in place. Hole Cutters are available in sixteen different sizes, from 3/4in to 2 3/8in. Carbide cutting edges will last a long time and will provide excellent service. Notice that the drilled-out slug in this photo has a very thin outer ring. This shows the kind of cutting edge these tools have; the outer circumference of each hole is the spot that receives the initial cutting force. This design helps the cutters drill clean holes with no vibration or rim scuffing.

WESCO Autobody Supply

WESCO is typical of most first-class autobody paint and supply stores. It carries a full line of automotive paint products, from primers to clearcoats. In addition, the store's inventory includes numerous autobody tools and supplies. There is a wide assortment of sandpaper grits in various-sized sheets that accommodate air files, rotary sanders, DAs, sanding boards, and other sanding tools. Safety equipment is also available, like filter masks, respirators, latex gloves, and painter's coveralls. Jobbers who work for autobody paint and supply stores are generally well versed in autobody and painting products. If you are confused about what types of products you need for your job, describe the type of work you are involved with so that they can help you.

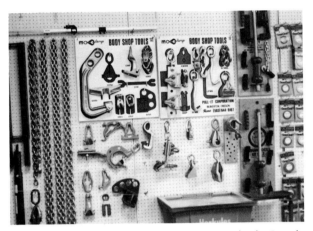

Like most of its counterparts, WESCO Autobody Supply carries a wide range of products aimed toward a market of professional autobody repair technicians and painters. For this reason, it stocks large tools designed for frame and body straightening, like the bodyshop tools shown here. To go along with much of this heavy equipment, heavy-duty anchors must be solidly set in floors to hold pressure pulling devices in place.

Lions Automotive

The R.B. Dent Puller's use is simple and straightforward. First, drill holes in strategic spots around the middle of dents. Insert a screw into the tool's collar and then tighten it into the newly drilled hole. Attach the screwdriverlike handle through the bar and tighten it against the collar. Then, place a 2x4 board under the dent puller for leverage and pull out dents while tapping their crowns with a body hammer. This tool was reportedly designed and first manufactured back in the 1950s and was used by professional bodyshop artisans through the 1960s and 1970s. The tool is simple and inexpensive and works as designed. Its 14in bar combined with a 2x4 board allows for plenty of leverage. The drilled holes will have to be welded closed when repairs are completed.

Harbor Freight Tools

To get started with autobody repairs, you will need some hand tools. The 7-Piece Body and Fender Set from Harbor Freight Tools is inexpensive and should serve you well. Hammers are used on one side of sheet metal while dollies are held firmly against the other side to act as mini-anvils. This set includes, left to right, a bumping hammer, pick and finish hammer, reverse curve hammer, double-ended hand dolly, shrinking dolly, curved dolly, and utility dolly. Not all hammer and dolly work is conducted like a hammer and anvil operation. Many times, especially with heavily creased dents, a dolly will be positioned away from immediate damage, more toward the center of dents. Outward pressure is put on the dolly as a body hammer is lightly but rapidly tapped along a dent's crown to help reduce dent depth. This work takes lots of practice to perfect.

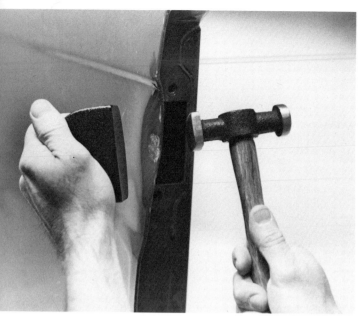

Here you see a utility dolly and bumping hammer in use to straighten a dent on this tailgate. A number of light, repetitive hammer taps will work much better than solid hammer blows. Working with different combinations of hammers and dollies will produce varying results. You must practice on an old door or fender before tackling this kind of work on your favorite car or truck.

Sunchaser Tools

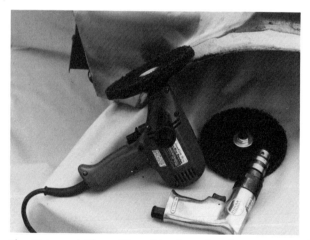

The Strip and Clean Fiber Disc from Sunchaser Tools is designed to remove paint, undercoating, surface rust, and plastic filler without clogging up and without removing metal. It has a 6in diameter and is 1/2in thick. This size is great for reaching into doorjambs, drip rails, and instrument panels and along body panel lines without cutting metal edges. For large, open panels, a maximum of 4500rpm is recommended. For reaching into limited access areas, use the disc on the end of a small air drill with a minimum of 1500rpm to 2500rpm. One disc should be able to completely strip two to three large fenders, and stripping a complete car body down to shiny bare metal may require up to seven discs.

The Friction System uses the Amazing Disc, which shrinks stretched metal back to its original flat contour. Dents must be worked out as much as possible before the disc's application. The concept is simple: heat the stretched metal until it turns blue, and then quickly cool it with a wet towel to shrink it back into shape. The problem has been, until now, that typical heating and cooling with a torch is not always safe and requires lots of patience and practice to master. The Amazing Disc, however, does not present the same safety problems as open flames, and it has the ability to find high points of stretched metal for the operator. The disc must be operated on a 3hp to 3.5hp heavy-duty grinder capable of 5000rpm to 6000rpm. The 9in stainless steel—like disc with a corrugated outer edge is worked over a repair area for only 2 to 3 seconds, just enough to visibly turn high spots a blue-hot color. A wet towel is placed on the hot spots to cool and shrink that stretched metal. The process is continued until repairs are flat. Of utmost importance are the size of grinder used, 2- to 3-second application times, and cooling with wet towels. The process works remarkably well and may even drastically reduce the need for plastic body fillers on thin-skinned automobiles. Operational instructions for the Amazing Disc are critical. When ordering your disc, ask for a training video, too.

The Eastwood Company

Suction Cups can be very useful in pulling out wide, shallow dents. In lieu of drilling holes for picks, autobody technicians may sometimes attempt to pop dents out with the pulling strength supplied by suction cups. Wet the base of these tools before placing them, to help the grips grab tighter. As you pull on a suction cup, light hammer taps along the dent crowns will often reduce pressure on the crowns and allow metal to spring back to its original shape. The chalk circle in this photo indicates a crown around a wide, shallow dent. Pressure pulled out on the suction cups combined with light hammer taps popped out this dent.

Although newer car bodies are made of sheet metal that is too thin to allow for much hot work on them, automobiles of the 1950s and earlier have plenty of thick sheet metal to support the hot work of the Body Solder Kit. An informative instructional book comes with this standard body solder kit, which also includes three paddles, a 1lb tin of tallow, 1lb of Tinning Butter, five acid brushes, two wood file holders, two English body files, and five sticks of body solder. Essentially, dents on bodies with thick sheet metal are bumped out as well as possible and then coated with solder. Heavy-duty English files are used to smooth repairs to perfection. The Coachbuilder's File, pictured here with a metal handle, is used to highlight the highs and lows on metal panels to indicate where more hammer and dolly work is needed. A turnbuckle adjustment allows users to curve files slightly for rounded filing work.

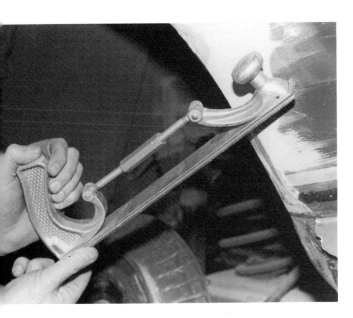

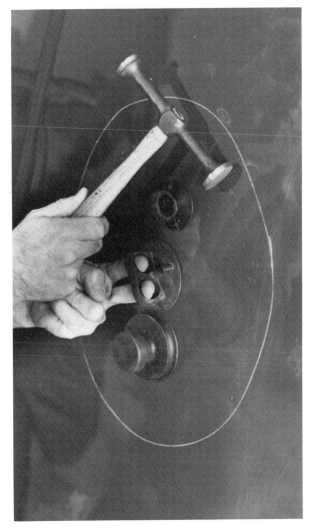

To begin pulling out this large dented area, Mycon could drill strategic holes in the quarter panel, insert a heavy-duty ¼in dent-pulling screw at the end of this Slide Hammer, and then use the 3lb Slide Hammer's grip to pound against the rear of the bar for the pressure needed to pull out parts of the dent. With optional accessories, the Slide Hammer from The Eastwood Company can be used for many purposes. To complement the screw tip, a hook, flange-type axle puller, and VISE-GRIP attachments are available. Combined with the power generated by the 3lb Slide Hammer, these accessories are able to perform many varied tasks.

The Body Man Tool comes in two sizes: a 12in bar and a small circular disc. Large self-tapping screws are found at the ends of these tools. A ⅜in drill is used to place a screw close to the center of a dent for the bar and on a small dimpled dent for the disc. Once the screw grabs hold, you slow down the drill speed and allow the dent to "walk" up the screw. Too much drill speed will cause the screw to strip out. As some metal is moved up, lightly tap the dent crown with a body hammer to help reduce metal tension and stress. As work progresses and metal starts to flatten out, stop the drill and use a wrench to put more stress slowly on the dent. When the screw is snug, pull back on the drill and again tap the dent crown. In no time, dents and dimples are pulled out. Be sure to weld the screw holes closed so that moisture is not permitted to begin a rusting process on the exposed metal edges.

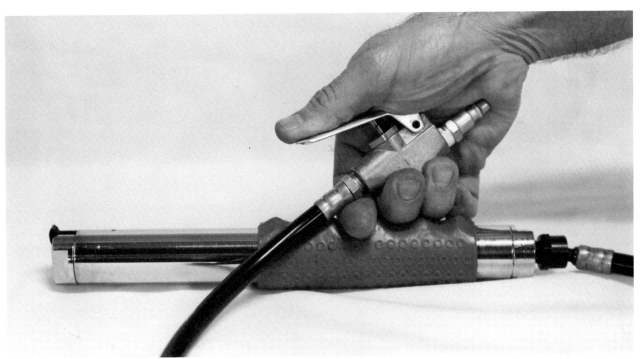

Reaching into confined spaces to bump out dents is nearly impossible in some cases. But, with the Air Pecking Hammer, you can remove dents and creases on door panels, fenders, rocker panels, and other hard-to-reach areas as small as 2in wide. Each time this tool's trigger is depressed, a small pointed hammer at the far end strikes one blow. Work out dents with patience and precision in areas you thought were totally inaccessible, like inside tailgates. A portion of this tailgate's skin was removed to demonstrate that as some parts are taken off of a panel—the tailgate latch, in this case—access is made for the Pecking Hammer. Your air compressor needs to supply 90psi for the Air Pecking Hammer to reach its peak performance.

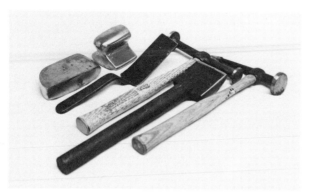

This body and fender tool assortment includes, left to right, the Heel Dolly, Heavy-Duty Dolly, Light Dinging Spoon, General Purpose Dinging Hammer, Spoon Dolly, and Sharp Point Finishing Hammer. Most autobody repairs will require an assortment of hand tools. As repairs start to flatten out metal, lighter hammer and dolly work is required. The point on a finishing hammer works much better than a blunt end on a general-purpose hammer in picking out tiny indentations and other small imperfections. This work of metal bumping takes practice. Note that the triangular-shaped area of white next to this hammer and dolly is plastic body filler. This part of the car had been repaired once before, unfortunately by someone who thought lots of body filler was better than meticulous hammer and dolly efforts. That material will be completely taken out and the entire area properly repaired before Mycon will allow this vehicle to leave his shop.

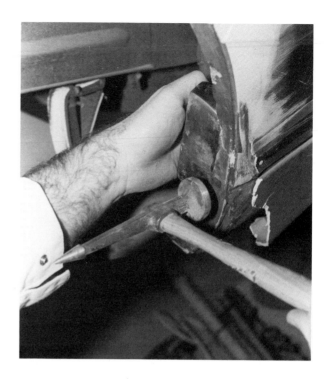

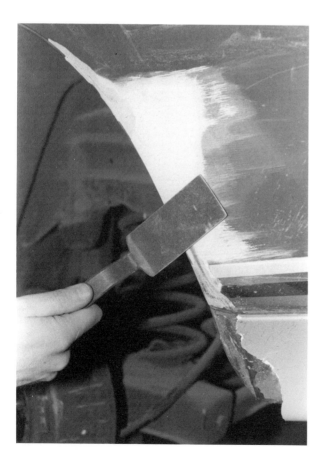

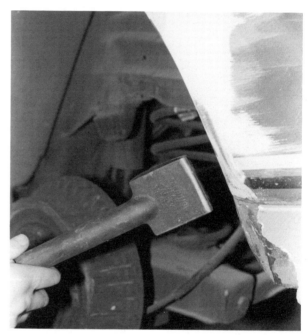

The Light Dinging Spoon, left, measures 2in by 4in. It is *not* a prying tool. Rather, it is used to spread body hammer blows across a wider area. Some technicians have even used it to slap very high spots in order to flatten them; this has been done lightly, as all hammer or striking work is done on sheet metal. The larger and heavier tool is called the Spoon Dolly. Its long extension handle can reach into inaccessible areas and be used as a striking tool or pry bar. Hand tools like these have been around the autobody repair business for a number of years. Most were originally developed by active repair people who had needs for tools of these dimensions and made prototypes themselves. Eventually, manufacturers got wind of these ideas and began producing them for everyone.

Sheet metal stretches when damaged in a collision. One main objective for autobody technicians is to shrink metal back to its original form. To help autobody repair people better accomplish their shrinking chores, Eastwood offers the Twist Hammer and Shrinking Dolly. The Twist Hammer shrinks metal in two ways: The striking head has sharp teeth shaped in a swirl pattern that grab stretched metal, and when this head strikes an object, an internal cam causes the head to rotate for even faster shrinking action. The Shrinking Dolly face is covered with serrations; combined with the action and grip of a Twist Hammer, these tools shrink stretched body panel areas. Note the swirling teeth marks from the Twist Hammer head on this painted fender area.

Working with the Twist Hammer and Shrinking Dolly, Mycon uses a pair of QUICK GRIPs to hold the fender secure on a portable stand. These locking tools work very well for a multitude of uses. The soft vinyl grip pads are safe to use on fiberglass panels and on other materials that would otherwise be scratched by metal clamp tools. When you tackle various autobody repair projects, take a few minutes to figure out how to make your work environment most comfortable. In this case, securing the fender in this manner made hammer and dolly work much easier to accomplish.

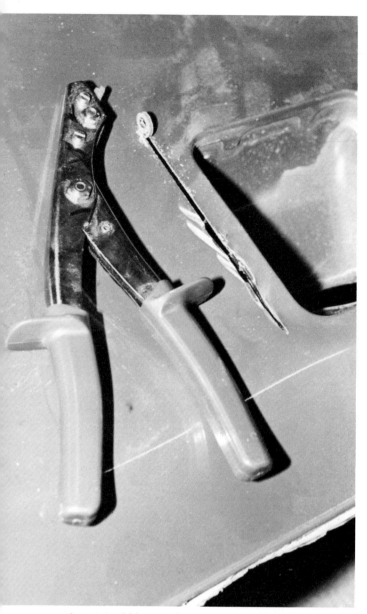

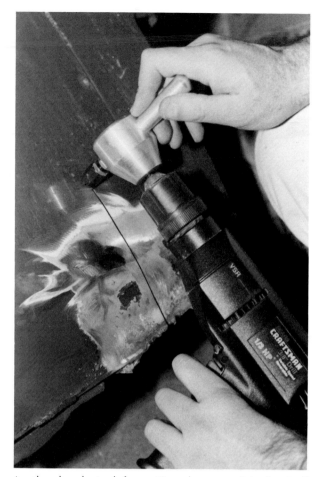

Another handy tool for cutting sheet metal is the Drill Nibbler. It is used with a power drill to cut through sheet metal quickly and easily. This tool can cut in straight lines or curves with no problems. The cut edges are clean, and the surrounding surfaces are not distorted. The Drill Nibbler can cut up to 18-gauge ($1/20$in) steel or aluminum. Cutting is accomplished by a reciprocating die that stamps out small metal chips. To start cuts in the middle of a panel, drill a $1/2$in hole for the cutting head. Each turn of a drill makes a clean cut with a replaceable steel cutting edge on the tool. The Drill Nibbler's no-slip hex drive also helps it to follow intricate patterns easily and cleanly.

The Mini Nibbler cuts through sheet metal without distorting surrounding metal. This cut was originally started at the bottom with a utility cutoff tool equipped with a grinding-cutting wheel; notice the jagged cut in comparison with the Mini Nibbler's. The Mini Nibbler's design incorporates two stationary jaws and a movable center blade. As metal is cut, scrap is rolled up from the center of the tool in a compact, out-of-the-way position. The jaws are made from heat-treated tool steel for long use and are replaceable. The Mini Nibbler can cut up to 15-gauge aluminum, brass, or copper and up to 18-gauge mild steel. Replacement jaws and center blades are available.

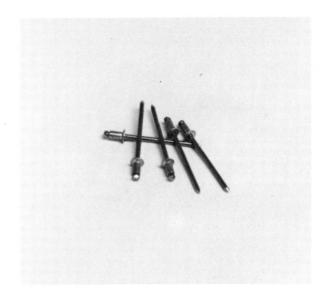

Drilling out spot welds is easy with the Spot Weld Cutter Assembly. The 1/4in arbor has an adjustable pilot so that you can set the depth of a cut by just a few turns with a hex key wrench, to drill through either both panels or the top one only. Its heavy-duty cutter has three large cutting teeth, and the hex shaft will not slip in your power drill chuck. Drill speed is 900rpm maximum. The cutting assembly is replaceable. This tool makes clean spot weld cuts to enable users to separate body panels for replacement. Remaining spot weld centers are removed with a grinder. For most applications, it is best to center punch spot welds before drilling.

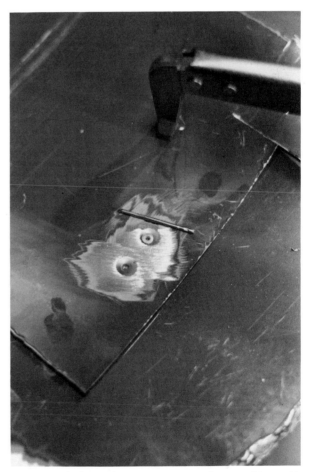

Countersunk Rivets have many uses when working with sheet metal. These 1/8in-diameter aluminum rivets are just the right length for joining two sheet metal panels together. For best results in having rivet head tops at or just below panel surfaces, use the Dimpling Pliers to initiate a slight dimple wherever rivet heads are to be set. Small coats of body filler will cover both dimples and rivet heads in one pass. Once an area is sanded and painted, repairs will not be noticed.

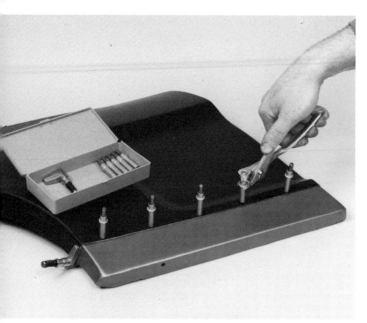

Installing new sheet metal skins is difficult when you do not have the means to secure them during welding maneuvers. This job is made easier with help from the Panel Holding System. To secure these blind holders, simply drill ⅛in holes through both the new skin edge and the existing sheet metal skin edge. Insert fasteners and then tighten them with special pliers. Each fastener has up to 20lb of holding power on each side of the hole. Side-grip fasteners grip tight for edge work and will not damage surfaces. Each set contains two side holders and ten blind holders.

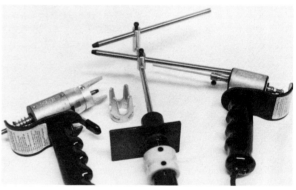

A great deal of sanding and grinding work is done when autobody repairs are made. The 36 Grit Sanding Disc does a great job of removing paint, surface rust, debris, and other material when used with a high-speed rotary sander. In addition, this tough sanding disc is also strong enough to smooth rough edges on sheet metal, especially sharp burrs like the ones at the base of this disc.

The Complete Eastwood Welding System enables users to braze, arc-weld, and spot-weld without additional complicated equipment. The 100amp welder operates off of standard 115volt household current; a 30amp circuit breaker or 20amp time delay fuse is required. Variable amperage control gives consistent output from 20amps to 100amps. The duty cycle is 20 percent to 100 percent, depending on the output setting. The machine will operate off of any AC electrode and will weld 16-gauge to ³/₁₆in steel. The spot weld accessory, at the far left in the second photo, attaches to the power unit's electrode holder. Its small size allows you to spot-weld repair panels, even in tight spaces. The spot welder works on 18- to 26-gauge sheet metal. A carbon arc torch, center, provides intense heat for bending, tempering, and brazing without the sometimes cumbersome setup of a gas torch set. On the far right is a stitch welder. Like the other tools, it connects to the power unit's electrode holder. This unit has a diode that essentially reduces output by half so that sheet metal can be safely welded. Along with the diode, the tool's pulsating action allows users to join metal as thin as 22 gauge.

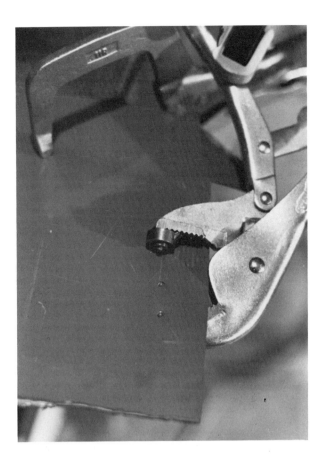

Lined up from left to right are Eastwood's MIG Edger, Panel Flanger, and Dimpling Pliers. These tools are useful during autobody repair operations that involve the welding or riveting of sheet metal panels. Finishing off welded body panels can be difficult owing to the differences in hardness between sheet metal and welding beads. Excessive grinding can weaken welded joints, and the resultant heat can warp panels. The MIG Edger crimps a 45-degree edge on both the existing body panel and the patch panel, as shown. The V made by this tool allows a space that is filled in by weld beads, to greatly reduce the amount of grinding that would be necessary to make patch finishes smooth. The Panel Flanger offers strong cam-action jaws that produce an offset lip along sheet metal edges up to 18 gauge in thickness. This is done so that replacement panels can fit flush next to the panel sections they will be welded to. This provides a strong joint that is easy to weld together. Dimpling Pliers put a countersunk dimple in sheet metal, as shown here, to allow rivet heads to remain intact after all grinding and filler chores have been completed. Line up your patch panel over the repair area and drill a series of ⅛in holes through both panels. Remove the patch panel and dimple each hole.

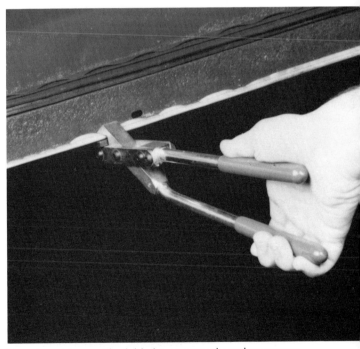

New door skins must be folded over correctly, or damage can be done to the outside faces. With the Door Skin Installer, that work is made easier. This tool has a 1½in-wide nylon pad that eliminates damage to door skin faces while crimping. Its 12in overall length offers excellent leverage, which, in turn, requires less operator effort.

The Eastwood 85amp Dual Purpose Wire Feed Welder is unique because it uses a special wire that has flux core and results in quality welds with little spatter or slag. It operates on standard 110volt, 20amp household current and accepts 4in or 8in wire rolls. This unit works well outdoors or in drafty areas where MIG welders would have a difficult time because their gas is blown away from work surfaces. It can weld sheet metal and heavier steel up to $^{3}/_{16}$in thick. Optional accessories include a gas conversion kit and aluminum wire drive adapter for MIG and aluminum welding. Safe welding includes making a solid ground with the heavy-duty clamp and wearing a welding hood with the appropriately numbered dark lens and heavy gloves. To keep welding nozzles in working order, use the MIG Tip Cleaner. It works much like the HTP Nozzle Reamer described in chapter five. Welding on sheet metal correctly requires practice. Too much heat will distort or burn through thin sheet metal, and too much welding material built up on the panels will require excessive grinding. The top and middle holes filled on this test panel have received far too much welding. The bottom hole was slowly built up through a series of three short burns. Each layer was completely cleaned of flux before the next weld, resulting in less welding material on the panel. The three short welding burns were cooled immediately to reduce the possibility of panel warp or distortion. This hole is in the process of being ground down and will soon make a good repair.

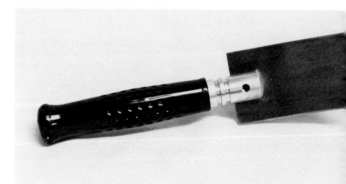

Filling in small holes, rips, or voids between panels, or on small metal parts, is a difficult operation because nothing is behind those areas to support welding material. The Welder's Helper is made of copper and can be placed behind these voids to act as a welding support. Once this tool is positioned behind a hole, simply weld the entire area, usually without stopping. After the repair is complete, remove the tool; it will not stick because it is made of copper. The Welder's Helper's patented design incorporates a heat sink principle to minimize surface distortion.

Never sand on autobody panels using sandpaper held in your hands alone. Hands are not flat, and their bony protrusions could cause slight sanding grooves on panels. Instead, rely on sturdy Sanding Blocks. Blocks, like this one, are available in different sizes to accommodate a wide range of uses. Made of hard rubber, this block offers a flat sanding surface and long slots for the insertion of sandpaper ends. Small brads inside the slots help keep sandpaper securely positioned.

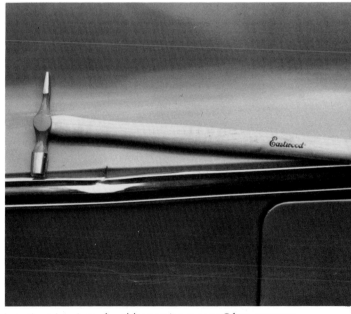

Locating trim pieces for older cars is not easy. Often, restorers are forced to repair trim that is in less-than-perfect condition. The Trim Hammer is an ideal size for lightly and gently pounding out dents on flat stainless trim. The face is good for dents on flat sections, and the cross peen is perfect for along edges and corners. The dropforged hammer head is hardened and tempered, weighs only 3½oz, and is 4in long. The hickory handle offers good strength with a comfortable balance and feel.

Chapter 7

Painting Equipment

Automobiles must be painted to keep their bodies from rusting away. That's the bottom line, and the original reason paint was applied to them decades ago. From that bottom line, it is easy to appreciate how automotive paint and related paint products have come such a long way in making our cars and trucks look so much better than they did with simple monotone black paint schemes, the only choice offered for many early automotive years.

The tens of thousands of automotive paint colors available today offer auto enthusiasts a huge selection of various paint schemes, blends, styles, and custom options that are limited only by the imagination. Proof of this is clearly evident at car shows and in auto magazines, which regularly present outstanding automobiles sporting beautiful and unique custom paint finishes ranging from one-color perfection to wild hue combinations all blended together in schemes any artist would envy.

Spray painting gorgeous and glossy finishes on cars requires much more preparation and attention to detail than does slapping paint on houses or storage sheds. The painting environment must be clean and dust free, masking applied meticulously, and application equipment in top condition. In addition, each step of car body preparation must have been completed without flaw if overall jobs are to result in finish perfection. Every project maneuver and preparatory task is just as important as the endeavors directly involved with the actual spray painting of the top coat. Specific requirements regarding the use and setting up of spray paint equipment must also be understood and implemented—like air pressure settings, air hose size, air dryer and filter specifications, dimensions of the air cap orifice on the spray gun, and so on.

Talk over your auto painting projects with a knowledgeable jobber at the autobody paint and supply store. Be sure the paint products you have chosen are compatible and that you completely understand all the application preparations and processes involved with the overall operation before spraying paint. In addition, automotive paint manufacturers provide auto paint stores with lots of information regarding the use of their products. This material is available to customers in the form of free informational sheets and application guidelines. Acquire the ones that relate to the products you plan to use, and refer to them for specific application instructions.

Snap-on Tools Corporation

The BF501 Spray Gun from Snap-on is a rugged and lightweight unit equipped with an all-purpose air cap enabling it to spray a variety of materials, including acrylic enamel, acrylic lacquer, urethanes, and base coats. It also features improved atomization for positive control of today's metallic paint products. Just below this large Spray Gun is a Detail Gun nozzle that sports its trigger lever on top of the assembly. A small paint cup, toward the upper right, attaches to this gun. Maneuverable Detail Guns are used for small painting tasks like spraying doorjambs, engine compartments, instrument panels, and so on. Surrounding the paint guns is an assortment of Air Dryers, Filters, and Pressure Regulators. For paint jobs to result in fine finishes, air supplies must be free from moisture and contaminants and must be delivered at prescribed pressure increments. All professional auto painters use such devices to ensure that the air supplies for their spray guns are pure and regulated according to paint manufacturer recommendations.

WESCO Autobody Supply

Every auto painter must regard the air supplies for spray paint guns with the utmost concern. Just a drop of water, a few pieces of dirt, or any amount of contamination will cause definitive blemishes on paint finishes. To avoid such problems, plan to install an air dryer–filter in-line between your air supply source and paint gun. At the least, use the Disposable Air Filter that is connected to the end of an air hose on one side and your paint gun on the other. This model is inexpensive and will hold up to 2 tablespoons of water. Typically, heat is created as an air compressor operates. This heat causes condensation to develop within the compressor's air supply system. As air travels away from a compressor in hose lines, it cools to form droplets of water. If not removed before reaching a paint gun, this moisture will be expelled along with air at the gun, to cause blemishes on paint surfaces.

Harbor Freight Tools

The Industrial Paint Spray Gun has been designed for autobody and industrial uses. It is equipped with a fine spray adjustment and a 1qt siphon cup that attaches to the gun with a camlock. The cup has a reinforced base and is Teflon lined. The recommended size for the air hose is $3/8$in, and for the air inlet $1/4$in NPT. This gun will spray paint at 30psi to 70psi and provide 11cfm at 50psi. As is typical with most spray paint guns, two adjustment knobs are featured at the top rear portion of the tool—under the operator's thumb in this photo. One knob controls paint volume flow, and the other adjusts the width of the paint spray pattern. The air cap assembly located on the nose of these types of paint guns is rotated to offer paint application in either a vertical or horizontal spray.

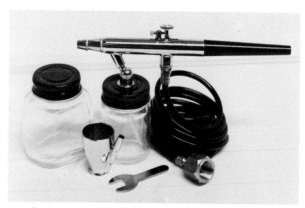

Although the Dual-Action Airbrush Set is quite similar to single-action types, a difference in the push-button trigger is noticeable. This trigger moves in two directions: down and back. The combination of these actions enables users to control and vary spray patterns while the tool is in use. Most professional artists use dual-action airbrushes for their ability to control paint intensity and cover large areas quickly. Quite simply, dual-action models give painters a lot more control and flexibility while painting, because they can use finger control to narrow paint sprays and then widen them, instead of having to move the entire airbrush away from the work piece.

Lions Automotive

Ordinarily, auto paint is stirred with a paint stick, although professionals also frequently rely on automated paint stirrers and shakers. Using a paint stick alone can sometimes result in heavier paint ingredients clinging to the bottom of paint cans, never to be thoroughly mixed as desired. The Pro-Paddle can solve inconsistent paint-mixing problems with its exclusive Magic Mix Tip. This brush tip will dislodge heavier paint pigment and metallic material from the bottom of paint cans to ensure their proper mixing. In addition, the Magic Mix Tip can also be used to clean paint can lids and rims so that all pigment ingredients are contained together as an effective mixture. Pro-Paddles are made of a heavy-duty, nonstick, chemical-resistant plastic that is easy to clean.

The Eastwood Company

To repair autobodies or ensure that some new paint finishes will cure with desired results, existing paint layers must be removed. Paint stripping can be accomplished through messy chemical strippers, coarse-grit sanding, or the use of special tools designed just for such tasks. The Flap Wheel removes paint, rust, and other surface coatings when applied with an electric drill or pneumatic tool to a maximum of 18,000rpm. It has a 3in diameter and 1in width and is mounted on a 1/4in shaft. Its design lets it reach into corners and recessed areas. Flap Wheels are available in 60 and 180 grits. Along with the Flap Wheel is the 5in abrasive Cleaning Disc. It is made of silicon carbon bonded together with long-lasting epoxy. This disc will clean metal fast without damage when used flat or on edge at slow speeds to a maximum of 5000rpm. Electric drills work well as long as only light pressure is applied, because it is the abrasive bits on the end of the fibers that beat and abrade surfaces clean. The Cleaning Disc is able to get into pits and slightly irregular surfaces to remove multiple coats of paint and light rust, although the tool is not recommended for extremely rough surfaces. Correct usage will result in finishes comparable to those sanded with 80-grit sandpaper.

Paint applied over rust spots may look decent for a while but will peel, crack, or chip in short order. All rust and corrosion must be removed before any paint is applied. For large jobs, regular rotary sanders or sandblasters can be used with great results. The Spot Blaster is a versatile and convenient tool for preparing small rusty spots for paint. It is a siphon blaster that has been designed with a unique venturi chamber and medium bag to capture and reuse 98 percent of its sandblasting abrasive. The tool operates at 90psi, and the bag holds enough abrasive to offer at least fifty shots before needing a refill. This unit comes standard with a 1½in diameter round adapter that is capable of cleaning areas about the size of a quarter dollar down to bare metal. Optional accessories include the edge adapter, which has an extended lip to fit over corners; a ½in diameter round adapter for small spots; the inside adapter for inside corners; and the outside adapter for cornered edges. The recycling feature of this sandblasting tool may justify the use of more specialized, effective, and expensive sandblasting abrasives, as it is designed to accommodate almost all media.

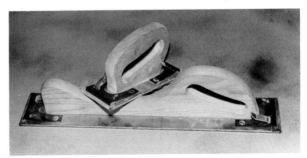

All sanding preparation for automotive paint applications must be done with tools, *not* bare hands. Paint finish quality is dependent upon proper surface preparation, as any imperfections will generally be magnified once paint finishes cure. To complement the use of DAs and other tools, Board Sanders work well during final sanding endeavors. These tools feature rubber-covered aluminum bases that sand surfaces flat and quickly highlight low spots and other problem areas. Handles are made of maple, are comfortable to use, and come in both long (16in) and short (4in) sizes. Both tools use standard 2¾in-by-17½in sandpaper sheets, cut to fit the small board.

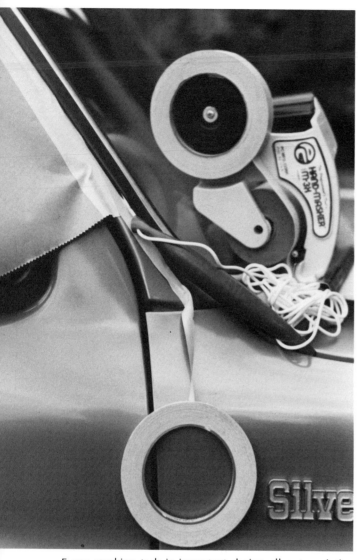

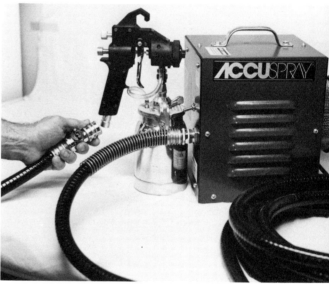

Every masking task is important during all auto painting endeavors. Just a small spot of overspray will generally offset an otherwise great paint job. One common area that shows blemishes of overspray is windshield trim moldings. To help painters mask around these moldings, Eastwood offers the Weatherstrip Masking Tool, seen in the foreground. This device lifts windshield molding edges off of surfaces while placing a vinyl cord under them. The cord holds the edges off of surfaces to allow plenty of room for placing masking tape under them. Once a strip of tape is attached to the bottom of the moldings with the adhesive side up, masking paper can be attached to it and then folded over the windshield. This results in complete masking of the molding edges. Another tool designed to make masking easier is the Hand-Masker Paper and Tape Dispenser. It will hold and cut paper rolls up to 9in wide and tape up to 1in wide. It automatically places tape along a paper edge so that each section pulled off the tool is ready for immediate application. This is a timesaver and work saver that eliminates the hassles associated with putting tape on paper separately after paper has been positioned. This tool also features a handy roller and cutting edge on top of its body for individual rolls of the 1/2in and smaller tape commonly used to outline intricate items before the application of wider paper-and-tape combinations.

Tighter regulations on the amounts of volatile organic compounds (VOCs) that are allowed to escape into the atmosphere during auto painting operations have brought about significant changes in the way paint is applied to cars and trucks. Some states require professional auto painters to equip their shops with expensive spray booths designed to capture and filter out a great quantity of VOC overspray pollutants. Paint manufacturers are busy developing and improving waterborne paint products that contain no VOCs, which are prevalent in the petroleum solvents—reducers and thinners—used in common paint products for autos. Another method of reducing paint overspray and VOCs is through the use of an HVLP spray paint system. Eastwood offers the AccuSpray System, which produces its own air supply and reduces paint overspray by up to 80 percent over that resulting from conventional high-pressure applications. The complete AccuSpray System includes a two-stage turbine air generator, 30ft of atomizing hose, a #11 gun with a 1qt cup, and a quick-disconnect coupling with a control valve. Paint overspray is reduced through this HVLP system because paint hits surfaces under a lower pressure, thus reducing the ricochet effects of paint particles. Users have in addition reported up to 25 percent reductions in the amount of paint normally needed for full autobody paint jobs. Eastwood also offers a three-stage HVLP system and an HVLP paint gun that uses compressed air.

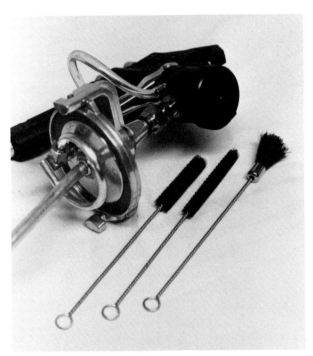

Automotive spray paint guns are high-precision tools. Slight scratches or other blemishes incurred on ports or passageways can disturb spray patterns to the point they are no longer usable. Paint guns must be thoroughly cleaned at the end of each painting session. To assist in your paint gun—cleaning efforts, use brushes specifically designed for that purpose. The Spray Gun Cleaning Set includes three different-sized brushes that will accommodate most gun-cleaning applications. Along with these brushes, be sure to consult cleaning guidelines included with your spray gun's operating instruction manual.

This is a complete set of Pinstriping Sword Brushes. The two on the left have recently been used and characterize what each brush looks like when wet. Clean and dry, bristles appear bushy. Each brush is designed for pinstripes of various widths. From left to right are #00 for very fine pinstripes, #0 for fine work, #1 for light lines, #2 for medium-width lines, #3 for heavy pinstripes, and #4 for bold lines. These pinstripe brushes come with individual capped storage tubes, as shown here. Pinstripe brushes are commonly referred to as "swords." They are designed to hold a lot of paint so that long pinstripes can be put on in one stroke. Many pinstripe artists lay down a line of thin Fine Line tape to use as a guide. Pinstripes are painted to within $1/8$in of the tape to ensure straightness. Pinstripe designs that entail curves and other patterns rely upon a painter's ability and artisanship.

An auto paint attribute that is a favorite among many auto enthusiasts is specialized paint lettering. The paintbrushes used for lettering are all designed for specific purposes. The Lettering Brush Outfit includes most of the brushes you'll need for almost any lettering job. From left to right are two Red Sable brushes used to produce fine, accurate lines for light scroll and signature work; three Brown Quill brushes for professional lettering applications; three Gray Quill brushes designed for beginners; and three Jet Stroke brushes that are big enough to hold lots of paint for filling in big, wide letters and accents.

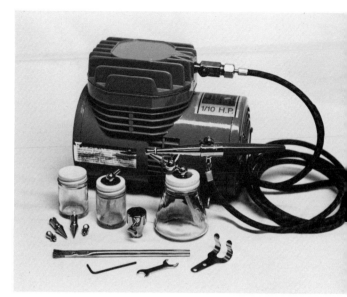

Enthusiasts who want actual painted pinstripes on their car or truck but lack the confidence to apply them with a brush should try the Beugler Professional Pinstripe Kit. The Beugler Kit is a unique tool that delivers paint by way of a small roller on the cap that lifts paint from the chamber to ensure crisp applications. The paint chamber employs a plunger mechanism that allows users to squeeze out excess air so that the wheel can lift paint consistently without frequent refills. The tool is precision made to within a tolerance of 0.002in, thus eliminating gaps and leaks. The fittings are so precise that a thin film of paint on a striping wheel actually acts as a lubricant. Each kit contains a standard set of seven wheel heads measuring $1/64$in, $1/32$in, $3/64$in, $1/16$in, $3/32$in, $7/64$in, and $1/8$in wide. Guide rods are also included; these attach to the top of the tool and are adjusted to follow along specific autobody lines or the optional Magnetic Pinstriping Guide Strip shown here. The Magnetic Guide Strip is a 15ft roll that secures to sheet metal and is adjusted for use as a straightedge guide. Guides are important when it comes to painting perfectly straight pinstripes. The Beugler can also be used freehand to paint curves and other pinstripe patterns. Optional wheel heads are available that include bold and double stripe models.

The Airbrush Set is used to produce special paint effects, from pencil-thin lines to smooth, uniform areas of color, with countless variations in between. They can also be used for fine touchup paint work. No doubt you have seen lots of airbrush work on custom automobiles, especially those that sport wildly colorful caricatures and landscapes. A familiar use of airbrushes at car shows in recent years is that of artists who airbrush outstanding auto renditions on tee shirts, caps, and other things. Airbrush units are powered by small air compressors. Paint is mixed in jars that are attached to the airbrush unit. A number of nozzles are available to provide a variety of paint sprays. Airbrush tools are available in both single- and double-action types. The single-action model displayed here simply requires the depression of a trigger button for broad spraying effects with water colors, dyes, lacquers, and oils. Paint flow is started as soon as the button is depressed. Color can be regulated for fine or coarse effects, but the spray pattern cannot be varied during a stroke, except by changing the distance between the airbrush and the painting surface. Single-action airbrushes are the simplest in design and have the fewest moving parts. Airbrush kits can be purchased with or without an air compressor.

The Eliminator is a special tool used to clean out chips and nicks on painted surfaces before the application of touchup paint. The Eliminator tip consists of a tight bundle of strong glass fibers that gives users a concentrated scrubbing power equal to hundreds of pounds per square inch. Thousands of glass fibers, each thinner than a human hair, reach into the smallest pockets of rust to scrub out corrosion, wax, and road film. All contaminants must be removed before paint is applied to blemishes, to ensure a repair with a quality finish. The Eliminator not only removes contaminants but also cuts down the gloss around paint chip edges. Each tool offers a comfortable and secure grip. The fiber tips will not slip back into their case, no matter how hard you press down on them, owing to a positive-lock design. Two refill cartridges are stored in the Eliminator's handle. The Eliminator can also be used to remove rust from chrome, tools, electrical contacts, cable ends, and lots of other items. You may in addition find that it comes in handy for cleaning intricate spots in preparation for welding or gluing and for detailing small items such as screw and bolt heads.

The Action ChipKit includes everything you will need to repair paint chips on your car or truck, except the paint. As soon as a chip is noticed, use the special clearcoat sealer to seal off the damage and prevent further rust or blistering. Once you are ready to repair paint chips, have the right paint color and this kit on hand. Use the Eliminator to clean the chips and then the plain paper matchsticks to apply the paint. Apply more than one paint coat, and allow the touchup to build up slightly higher than the surrounding paint surface. When the paint is dry, according to the paint container's label, use the flexible, specially sized sanding block with two matched types of fine sandpaper sheets for automotive polishing in sequence to remove touchup paint build-up and make a smooth, scratch-free surface. With that task complete, apply ultrafine compound to bring back a mirror finish to the repaired area. The microfine polishing papers and compound in the Action ChipKit also work very well for moving surface abrasions, black rub marks, and even slight scratches and blemishes from painted surfaces.

Chapter 8

Detailing Equipment

Automobile detailing entails a series of processes that are undertaken for the express purpose of making cars and trucks look their absolute best. One critical element of auto detailing involves cleaning. The mere act of cleaning every square inch of an automobile will do wonders to improve its interior and exterior appearance. Combine that effort with some polishing, waxing, and dressing, and vehicles can be made to look better than new.

A great deal of detailing work must be done by hand; it just cannot be escaped. Bare hands alone cannot accomplish much, of course, so, at the least, detailers need water, soap, a wash mitt, and soft cotton towels or cloths. Believe it or not, a tremendous amount of detailing can be accomplished with just these supplies. Add a few things to the list—like a scrub brush, a floppy paintbrush, an old soft toothbrush, a pad of steel wool, and a few other simple items—and your detailing abilities will expand. To be sure, you'll need the basics of soap, water, and a wash mitt regardless of accessories, but the addition of helpful tools will assist your detailing-cleaning endeavors in speed, degree, and overall outcome.

After your car or truck has been meticulously scrubbed inside and out, from top to bottom and side to side, you'll be ready to enhance its squeaky clean appearance with various polish and wax products, conditioners, and protectants. Once again, most of these detailing chores can be accomplished with soft, clean applicators but the addition of a few simple tools will help work progress at a better rate. A soft brush for working conditioner into tires, for example, will help to give them a rich luster appearance that is complete and evenly finished. A soft toothbrush works well to remove polish or wax build-up along trim, badges, and moldings, and cotton swabs are ideal for applying protectant on vinyl panels around intricate metal obstructions.

Automobile detailing, regardless of tool accessibility, requires a lot of elbow grease. Although you can accomplish a great deal with a minimum assortment of tools like those just described, why do all of that work by hand alone? Unless you are determined to do it all the hard way, realize that a number of various tools are available that will help your auto detailing

efforts progress much faster, easier, and probably more efficiently.

The key to detailing with power tools is focused around the potential damage these machines can cause. Perhaps the most obvious example could rest with buffers-polishers. These tools do a fantastic job of bringing old paint back to life, but only if they are used correctly. Too much buffer pressure applied on top of ridges or next to painted indentations can quickly

California Car Cover Company

Meticulous car people have traditionally been leery of anything designed to be passed over the painted surfaces of their automobiles. Anything that could possibly cause scratches or swirls is taboo. This means that about the only way to get dust off of their cars has been to break out the soap, water, and soft cotton wash mitt every time—until now. The California Car Duster is a specially treated cotton fiber tool made to lift dust off of car surfaces without any chance of scratching paint. The design allows users to dust cars over and over again; in fact, the dirtier the tool gets, the better it works. The manufacturer recommends using this tool for a year or two before washing it. Instructions for its use are explicit and cover washing procedures for the tool itself. Apply the duster lightly, and only allow the end of the cotton fibers to touch painted surfaces. Downward pressure is neither recommended nor necessary. The California Car Duster comes with its own carrying case for convenient storage.

remove layers of paint down to primer or bare metal, resulting in paint burns. Other tools can also cause damage when not handled according to directions or when applied too aggressively.

Therefore, take advantage of the detailing tools at your disposal, but pay strict attention to their intended use, operational capabilities, and, most important, label or instructional safety recommendations. Then, be sure to clean and store tools appropriately so that they will be ready for detailing the next time you want to use them.

Empire Brushes

The stout-bristled Scrub Brush will do a good job of cleaning tires, especially when combined with a powerful soap or cleanser. This brush features strong plastic bristles that reach inside the grooves and letters on tire sidewalls to dislodge stubborn dirt accumulations. In clean condition, this brush also works well for scrubbing and shampooing neglected upholstery, convertible and vinyl tops, and a host of other unpainted or polished attributes. For those with recreational vehicles (RVs), trailers, or pickup trucks, the Vehicle Washing Brush is equipped with soft bristles and a vinyl bumper that absorbs shocks and protects vehicles from scratches. The wide bristle base works very well for cleaning RV and trailer siding, pickup truck beds, and unpainted running boards. Equipped with a threaded or tapered handle, this brush can be used to reach roof accessories on large vehicles that are normally positioned too high out of reach.

Makita U.S.A.

Black and Decker

The #9207SPC 7in Electronic Sander-Polisher from Makita comes standard with an abrasive disc, rubber mounting pad, locknut, locknut wrench, side handle, and spanner wrench. It is a variable-speed machine that can deliver from 1500rpm to 2800rpm. The electronic speed control will maintain a constant speed for maximum power and production. The tool weighs 7.7lb and is 18$\frac{1}{2}$in long. Equipped with a wool bonnet, it will make the task of polishing oxidized paint surfaces much easier and faster. The type of polish used with this machine is an important concern. Heavy-grit polishes designed solely for hand application must not be used with a power buffer. The combination of heavy grit and a high-rpm polisher will surely result in far too many paint burns and blemishes. You must read labels on polishes you intend to use to see if they are designed for machine application. Typically, products for machine application will contain less grit to compensate for the power being applied by machines. If you are confused about the proper type of polish to use with your polishing machine, or buffer, consult with a jobber at an autobody paint and supply store.

Serious auto detailers are equipped with a quality vacuum. The Model #6633 Black and Decker Wet/Dry Vac is a top-of-the-line, heavy-duty, 10gal vacuum capable of picking up all kinds of debris, dirt, and grit, as well as shampoo and water. Its large capacity is complemented with a 1.7hp motor that can move 102cfm. Standard equipment includes the hose, 6in gulper attachment, 10in metal crevice tool, washable cloth filter, bag, bag stretcher, and polyfoam secondary filter. The Wet/Dry Vac is useful in cleaning interior and trunk carpeting, of course, but is also valuable for picking up stagnant water from manifolds after engine cleaning, removing most of the shampoo and water from upholstery cleaning, removing papers and debris from along the interior base of windshields next to the dashboard, and performing a host of other tasks.

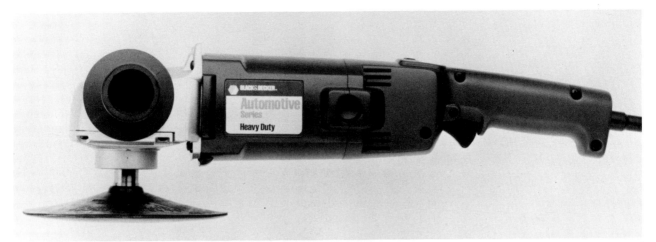

Except for the most meticulous, many detailers and auto enthusiasts use a buffer for polishing vehicles that have neglected and oxidized paint finishes. The BuffMaster Electronic Polisher from Black and Decker is a heavy-duty buffer that can provide a variable speed from 1500rpm to 3000rpm. It has a strong (8amp) motor and a convenient lock-on button. Access is provided for easy brush replacement, and the tool will accommodate 7in or 9in buffing pads. Caution must be exercised when using power buffers. The rapid head speed is always enough to rip off side trim and whip radio antennas into an operator's face. The pads can also burn paint if not maneuvered properly. Paint burns are caused when buffers are left to spin on only one spot, forced into corners, or left on top of ridges long enough to allow the pad to wear through paint layers down to primer or bare metal. An assortment of buffing pads are available at autobody paint and supply stores. Basically, one would use a *cutting pad* with certain polishes to remove oxidation and impregnated dirt from paint to bring back a shiny paint finish. Then, one would use a *finishing pad* with a mild creamy wax to remove any swirls or light spider webbing left behind by previous aggressive buffing. Those with little experience using buffers should not allow machines to exceed 1700rpm to 2000rpm.

The Chamberlain Group

The WAXMASTER 900 is a random orbital machine for polishing and waxing that can save you a great deal of work and also alleviate problems associated with high-speed buffers and paint burning. Since it operates in an *orbital* manner, the possibilities of tearing off trim and molding are greatly reduced. This machine features a quiet direct-drive motor and a contoured comfort-grip handle with push-button control. After working in polish and wax, it takes off dry residue if you remove the soiled bonnet and put on a clean one. When jobs are done, put the bonnets in your washing machine for cleaning. This is a machine that offers gentle polishing and waxing.

To complement its WAXMASTER orbital waxer and polisher, The Chamberlain Group offers Polishing Solution and Professional Wax designed for use with its machine. Polishing Solution is safe for all finishes, including clearcoats. It removes road films, dirt, grime, and oxidation, to leave behind a rich, hard shine ready for wax. This special formula goes into paint pores to hide slight scratches and imperfections and contains carnauba wax for durability and resistance to detergents. Professional Wax contains natural carnauba wax and nonabrasive cleaners that buff to a high gloss to protect and enhance paint finishes. It will protect against dust, dirt, sand, air pollution, and road grime.

Dremel

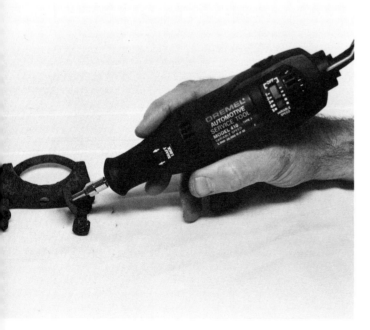

The Dremel Model 410 Automotive Service Tool comes in a kit that includes twenty-four accessories and bits for cutting, grinding, cleaning, sanding, polishing, drilling, sharpening, slotting, and much more. The tool has been engineered for rugged use and years of dependable service. Its shatter resistant housing sports a comfortable grip to provide precise fingertip control. A keyless chuck attachment allows fast replacement of bits. The variable-speed control is smooth and will adjust the tool speed from 5000rpm to 30,000rpm. This option lets users select which speed is best for a project. Many automotive stores have the *Dremel Bit Selection Guide Book* handy so that you can select optional bits to meet your automotive needs. This tool is handy and can be used for many tasks, from cleaning battery terminals with a wire wheel and polishing small auto attributes to cutting sheet metal and smoothing small sections of body filler. It can also maneuver into tight spaces where other tools could never fit.

TiP Sandblast Equipment

Serious detailing work requires close examination of all vehicle attributes. All too often, these inspections locate small spots of rust or other surface imperfections. Paint, rust, and contaminants must be removed from base materials before touchup paint can be applied. Jobs like this are custom-made for the US-10 Spot Blaster. This tool comes with a special abrasive called US FAST CUT. It is designed to remove surface materials and contaminants in seconds. The tool features a pliable and durable rubber boot that conforms to most surface contours and confines blasted spots to about the size of a U.S. quarter. Abrasive is automatically recycled into the attached bag for dust-free sandblasting. Standard accessories include a nozzle, a hex key, a wrench, and 1pt of US FAST CUT abrasive, enough for over 500 blasts. With intermittent use, this tool can be operated by as small as a 1hp air compressor.

The Eastwood Company

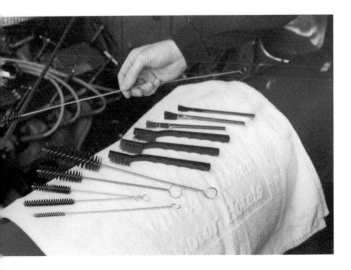

Engine detailing finds technicians faced with myriad recessed areas, nooks, crannies, and other small spaces to clean. Fingers are almost always too big to fit into these areas, especially when draped with a rag or cleaning cloth. Power washer pressure is often too strong for these cleaning tasks, and detailers are generally left scratching their head, trying to figure out how to clean these hard-to-reach spaces. The solution is brushes—an assortment of them. Not every brush is capable of cleaning every odd-shaped recess, nor are their bristles appropriate for every cleaning chore. The long-handled Engine Cleaning Brushes are designed for cleaning out the ports and passages of engine blocks during rebuilding, but they also do a great job during engine compartment cleaning. The Brass, Stainless, and Plastic Brushes that look sort of like toothbrushes also have their purposes. Use the Brass Brushes for cleaning soft metals, the Stainless Brushes for cast iron, and the Plastic Brushes for other unpainted surfaces. Small paintbrushlike brushes are great for working in solvent around recessed bolts and around carburetors. Small brushes have many uses in addition to detailing engine compartments. Consider having two sets: one for dirty and greasy engine work and another for relatively clean interior tasks. Be sure to clean brushes thoroughly after each use in order for them to be ready the next time something requires their scrubbing power.

The convenience of an aerosol is frequently thwarted when the supply of material in the can is gone and you don't have a fresh can handy. To solve problems like this, consider using a refillable sprayer like the Sure Shot from Eastwood. Although *not* designed for spraying paint, these units can be used to spray solvents, dyes, rust-inhibiting solutions, and almost any liquid with a viscosity of up to 10 SAE. The shelf life of most unpressurized chemicals is much longer than that of aerosols, so it may be wise to purchase required liquid products in quart, gallon, or large bulk containers and then apply them with one of these sprayers. Units are filled through a top-mounted capped opening and then charged with 90psi to 150psi from your air compressor. Along with the close-mounted nozzles, extension wands of 3in and 12in are available, as show here. When filled with solvent, these tools are ideal engine detailing tools, especially when neglected engine compartments are full of grease and grime build-up.

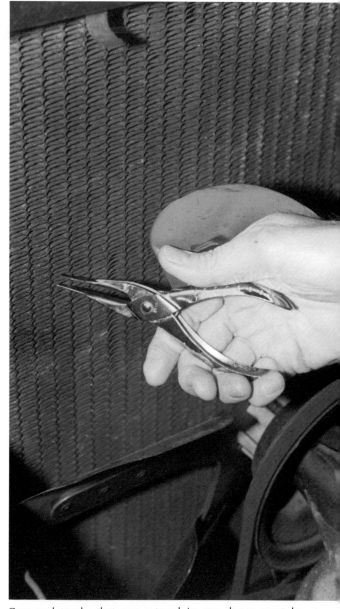

Cars and trucks that are entered in car shows must be meticulously detailed. Concours d'elegance competitions are even more critically judged, especially those for particular makes only, where judges are experts on the type of car in attendance. In-depth detailing for specific concours events goes far beyond so-called simple cleaning, polishing, and conditioning. The intense judging that competitive concours automobiles typically undergo includes alignment of their radiator fins. Any abnormality caught by a judge's eye will immediately cause a reduction in point value, and you can bet that a group of bent radiator fins will stand out like a sore thumb. Straightening out radiator fins is easy with Eastwood's Radiator Fin Pliers. This lightweight tool has teeth that are slim enough to fit easily within fin openings and wide enough to bend fins back evenly to their original position.

Air conditioning condensers feature a different fin pattern than regular engine radiators. The fins are lined up straight across, with coils buried in the middle. Case was thrilled when he saw this Fin Rake for the first time. He immediately popped open the hood of his 1981 Ferrari 308 GTSi and began straightening bent condenser fins. This tool features a series of teeth widths to accommodate any variation of condenser fin placement. A screwdriverlike handle makes the application of the tool easy in most cases. It can easily be removed, however, so the rake is more maneuverable in tight spaces, like this one in Case's 308.

Automobile glass is subjected to the same kinds of harsh road abuse as other vehicle attributes. At times, it can sustain wiper haze, hard water stains, and slight scratches caused by all sorts of conditions. The Professional Glass Polishing Kit combines a special wheel and compound like those used by specialty glass shops to remove such blemishes. Designed for use with a slow-speed (1500rpm) polisher equipped with a $5/8$in-by-11in standard thread or electric drill and its own standard $1/4$in adapter, this tool will do an excellent job of clearing most neglected glass to like-new condition. It will not, however, generally remove scratches that can be caught with a fingernail. The polishing wheel is $2^7/8$in in diameter and $1^1/2$in thick, plenty stout enough to complete fifty or more glass-polishing jobs. The compound that comes with the kit is a special cerium oxide that is mixed with water to develop a slurry. Each kit includes a wheel, a $1/4$in drill adapter, and 1lb of polishing compound. Note: Polishing glass is a messy job, and you should be prepared with adequate clothing and eye protection. Likewise, plan to wash your car or truck afterwards.

The left side of this plastic headlight cover looked just like the right side before it was restored with the Plastic Polish Kit. This hand application finishing kit utilizes a series of nine different pieces of cushioned and cloth-backed abrasives from 1500 to an amazing 12,000 grit. Used along with cleaners and a foam-backed block, this kit will enable you to restore many concave and odd-shaped plastic parts back to their original clear condition. The key to the success of this kit is in its extrafine-grit polishing sheets and compound. The foam-backed polishing block helps to maintain a flat polishing plane, too. Use the kit to polish all plastic lens attributes, including colored models.

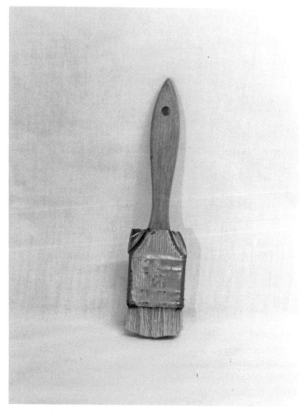

Common paintbrushes are exceptional tools for any auto detailing job. Wide, long, natural-bristled paintbrushes do a fantastic job of cleaning between wheel spokes, grille sections, moldings, and other hard-to-reach places. One should always use a cotton wash mitt for every car- and truck-washing endeavor. Small paintbrushes are sometimes ideal for reaching into louvered sections, around light housings, and so forth. Cut the bristles of a narrow (1in to 2in) paintbrush down to a 1/2in to 3/4in length, and the tool will be perfect for dislodging and whisking away dried polish and wax residue from lettering, trim, and badges. Be sure to use natural-bristled paintbrushes for your auto detailing needs, as synthetics may tend to cause minor swirl and spider web blemishes. It is wise to wrap a thick strip of heavy-duty duct tape around the metal bands of paintbrushes. The tape will cushion these bands and prevent scratches.

Chapter 9

Accessory Items

Automobile restoration, repair, paint, detail, and general workshops are usually equipped with a lot more tools, equipment, and devices than the bare necessities required for whatever specific work is performed at that location. Some people may refer to supplemental items as "goodies" or handy gadgets, whereas others might rely on the convenience these accessories offer to help make their work place efforts more efficient and manageable.

This chapter is filled with a potpourri of items that may not necessarily fit into specific tool or equipment categories but, nevertheless, could be valuable assets to auto enthusiasts in need of auto products capable of providing various types of service. In addition, let's not forget that automobile repairs and adjustments are frequently made away from garages and workshops in breakdown situations out on the road. During these frustrating times, it is nice to have a small toolbox that is tucked away in the trunk or under a seat and equipped with multiple service tools that can be used to tighten fasteners, reroute hoses, secure wires, hold parts to brackets, change tires, and so on. A handy light would be most helpful at night, and a few spare parts like belts, fuses, light bulbs, and hoses could be lifesavers when your car is broken down a long way from home.

Many tools and pieces of equipment—like soft-surfaced vise jaws and floor jack pads—are designed to work with other service items to complement their overall performance. Some products are designed for sharpening tools, and others are made for the purpose of storing and protecting tools and equipment when not in use. The automotive service market is flooded

Parking Solutions

Are you an avid auto enthusiast or restorer with too many vehicles and not enough indoor parking space? Those problems could be solved with the Parking Solutions Lift. Two lifts could easily turn a residential two-car garage into a four-car facility or help out a restorer by providing a storage place for project vehicles that is off the working floor and will also allow room for parking other vehicles underneath. These units can well serve enthusiasts in need of a lift for servicing or repairing auto undercarriages. Three Parking Solutions Lifts are available: a full sized lift with a capacity of up to 7,000lb, a midsized lift with a capacity of up to 4,000lb, and a sports car lift with a capacity of up to 3,000lb. Unit options include a choice of two platforms with steel diamond plates or one designed for heavy-duty wood planking. Steel drip pans can be ordered that will protect cars on the bottom from oil drips falling off cars on top. The company points out that regular support rails for garage doors and automatic opener motors can be adjusted or relocated to accommodate these lifts. A definitive twelve-step self-setup procedure shows how two people can install a lift in one day with help from a third person for about 10 minutes. The midsized and sports car models need no special equipment for their installation, but the full-sized model will require an engine hoist or fork lift to raise its one-piece welded platform.

119

with countless products all advertised to give consumers any number of means to make their auto repair or restoration efforts easier, faster, and more efficient. Most of these items work as expected and save professional and do-it-yourself auto people a lot of time, energy, and frustration.

Your accessory tool and equipment needs must be justified with regard to the service offered as compared against the price paid for the product. In other words, it may not be feasible for you to spend thousands of dollars on one item that will only save you a few minutes' work. Conversely, if that tool or equipment piece can perform vital functions over and over again, it may easily save you much more than its initial investment by reducing the amount of time that you would have to spend doing the same jobs without it.

Chief Automotive Systems

Chief's C.A.T. Cart II enables one person quickly and safely to move disabled vehicles and those that have been dismantled for restoration purposes. Units are equipped with two 12volt deep-cycle batteries that are wired in series for 24volt output. Batteries provide plenty of power for lifting and towing, even on inclines with up to 4 percent grades. A remote charger that is also included keeps the C.A.T. Cart II batteries charged. Vehicles are lifted with either a sling attachment or the optional Chief Wheel Lift System. Units have a 2³/₄in ground clearance and lifting heights of up to 16in. Front and back brakes are standard. The wheel track is 30in, and the wheelbase is 36in. Electric-hydraulic drives have two forward and two reverse speeds. An optional set of jumper cables enables operators to use these units as portable power carts for jump-starting vehicles.

Eagle Equipment Company

Along with wheel alignment lifts, tire changing units, wheel balancers, and brake lathe stations, Eagle Equipment offers this Pro-Lift Model SR-7AC above-ground automobile lift. Each Pro-Lift uses dual hydraulic cylinders combined with high-tensile strength leaf-chain. The design provides maximum lifting capability and safety with minimal maintenance. Lift pads are only 2½in high to allow the lifting of automobiles with flat tires or those with modified or lowered suspensions. The SR-7AC has a lifting capacity of 7,000lb and maximum lifting height of 78in. The unit's overall height is 147in, the overall width is 126in, and the working width between posts is 96in. A mechanically operated, spring-loaded lock is continuously engaged to offer maximum safety. Additional Pro-Lift models offer greater lifting capacities and working widths. Eagle Equipment even carries a Mobile Lift, which looks like a small forklift and can safely lift cars or trucks that weigh up to 7,000lb.

Bug Brick Products

Road film and bug residue glide off windshields with ease when they are cleaned with the Bug Brick and water. This inexpensive item removes stubborn grime and other deposits quickly and safely from glass, chrome, and other *unpainted hard surfaces*. The Bug Brick is made of a microcellular plastic foam that forms thousands of cutting edges to gently shave foreign matter off of surfaces when applied with just a small amount of water. Using a Bug Brick will prevent disgusting material from getting on your hands or imbedded in your wash mitt while you are cleaning dirty windshields and chrome bumpers. It will not absorb water or other liquids and is easy to rinse clean and store. Bug Bricks are *not* recommended for any painted or plastic surfaces.

Jericho Products

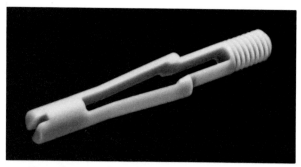

Installing oil pans without disturbing gaskets is easy with Oil Pan SnapUps. Since oil pans are generally awkward to maneuver, especially when you are lying on your back in cramped spaces, it is difficult to set them in place perfectly each time without gaskets sliding out of position and getting in the way of bolt holes. The slightest irregularity in the seal of an oil pan gasket will almost always result in oil leaks. Oil Pan SnapUps help to ensure gaskets are not disturbed by providing long stems that will guide oil pans into exact position every time. Simply screw SnapUps into the oil pan bolt holes in the engine block, position the oil pan in line with the stems, and then push the pan up against the engine block until it snaps in place. As bolts are installed around the oil pan, SnapUps are unscrewed and removed.

O.C.S. Shark File Sharpening System

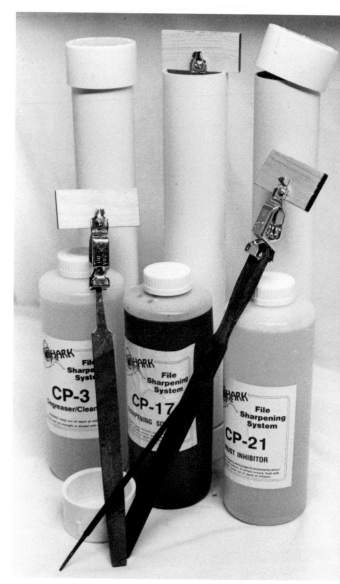

Files are great tools for removing burrs and sharp edges from metal and also do a good job of sharpening all sorts of implements as long as they are themselves kept sharp. An easy way to sharpen files is with the O.C.S. Shark File Sharpening System. Three separate solutions are used to sharpen files numerous times, extending their usability for up to five times their normal working life. Clean files first by hand and then with a card file, wire brush, or wire brush wheel to remove grease, glue, and impacted debris residue; all imbedded material must be removed to ensure optimum sharpening results. Then, according to definitive instructions, use a handy clipped hanger to suspend files in the CP-3 Degreaser/Cleaner solution poured into one of the standard kit tubes. After allowing files to soak in CP-3 the recommended amount of time, rinse with water, dry, and then immerse in a solution of CP-17 Sharpening Solution. After the recommended time has passed, remove files and rinse thoroughly with water. Once dry, soak them in the CP-21 Rust Inhibitor solution to provide them with corrosion protection.

Haack Products

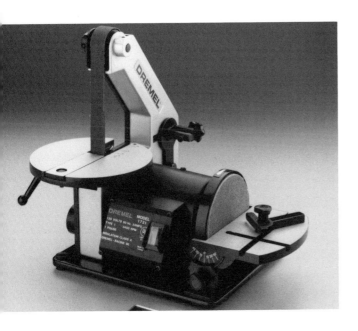

Mr. Wringer is a hand-operated tool used to squeeze water out of towels, chamois, and other wet cloths. It is lightweight and portable and can be mounted on things such as large sinks and benches. Rollers self-adjust for fabric thickness and are grooved for additional traction on wet materials. The unit weighs only 3.5lb and measures 17½in by 13in by 4in. It requires little or no maintenance and provides a level of service that is the same as or better than that experienced with old-fashioned washing machine wringers. This product could serve a variety of needs, especially for detailers who wring out cleaning cloths and drying towels regularly.

Dremel

SEFIDCo Tool Products Group

Sharp drill bits are easier to work with and much more efficient overall than dull ones. The Drill Bit Sharpener from SEFIDCo Tool Products Group takes the guesswork out of drill bit sharpening with its built-in guide angles. The unit attaches to any power drill for fast and accurate drill bit sharpening. The shaft of this sharpener's grinding wheel is secured in a drill motor chuck, and the tool will sharpen bits sized from 1/16in to 1/2in. It will sharpen cutting edges and remove high heels in high-speed steel bits up to 1/2in in diameter. This tool is portable and can be carried or stored almost anywhere. Operating instructions are complete and concise. While using this grinding tool, be sure to wear eye protection.

The Dremel #1731 Disc/Belt Sander can be useful for a wide variety of auto repair, detailing, and restoration operations. It can sand, deburr, polish, and finish metal, plastic, wood, and ceramic materials, making it perfect for restorers of antiques and classics with lots of wood attributes. The tool can also sharpen many objects. With the optional Drill Bit Sharpener, you can sharpen drill bits with diameters of from 1/8in to 1/2in. This is both a belt sander and a disc sander in one bench-top unit, and it has a lockable on-off switch with dust resistant cover, rubber insulation pads for smoother and quieter operations, a standard vacuum hose outlet for dust collection, a sturdy diecast aluminum housing, a belt-tracking and tension control mechanism, and more. Included with the Disc/Belt Sander as standard accessories are a miter gauge, an 80-grit sanding belt, an 80-grit sanding disc, a hex key wrench, and an instruction manual.

Black and Decker

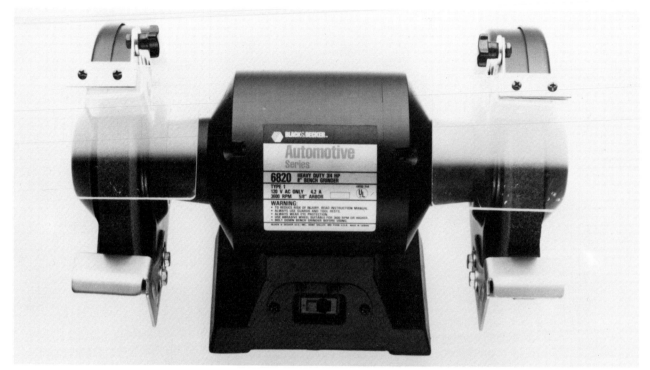

The Black and Decker 8in Bench Grinder can be used for a wide range of operations, from grinding part edges down for an appropriate fit to deburring freshly cut brackets. This unit features a 0.75hp sealed induction motor that delivers 3600rpm. Extrawide guards accept wire brushes used for myriad cleaning and rust removal tasks. Adjustable tool rests and protective eye shields allow for comfortable, safe, and efficient working conditions. The rear-exhaust design keeps material clear of users, and the heavy-duty cast-iron motor housing makes for excellent durability and tool longevity. Two grinding wheels are standard with this model: one medium and one coarse. Among the optional accessories available for this grinder are general (0.014in-diameter), high-speed buffing (0.0118in-diameter), and fine finishing (0.006in-diameter) wire brush wheels; an assortment of cotton buffing wheels; a wheel dresser; a cutter set; and more.

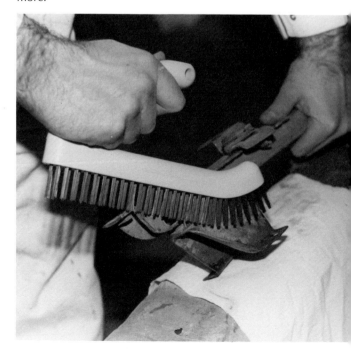

Empire Brushes

Wire brushes are used to clean slag from fluxed welding operations, scrub rust and scale from part surfaces, and perform a host of other cleaning chores. Typically, wire brush designs are such that knuckles and fingers are prone to accidental bumps, abrasions, and cuts. With the uniquely raised handle on the Wire Brush model from Empire Brushes, those worries are just about negligible. This brush shape also features an angled front nose section that works well for many tasks involving awkwardly shaped objects like this seat bracket assembly. The handle design not only gets fingers and hands away from work surfaces, it also affords a lot of extra brushing leverage, especially along bristles located directly below a user's hand.

Aeroquip Corporation

Steel braided hoses and anodized fittings are popular among street rod, hot rod, pro street, and other auto enthusiasts. Putting braided hoses and anodized connections together, though, can sometimes bring up problems of how to hold them secure while tightening. To help solve this problem, Aeroquip Corporation has developed Vise-Jaw Inserts especially made for the assembly of steel braided hoses and anodized connections. These inserts firmly hold the hex portion of fitting connections without marring their anodized finish. They are made of aluminum and can be used with any sized fitting from -03 to -32. The horizontal pocket pictured here is ideal for securely holding steel braided hoses while they are cut. Vise-Jaw Inserts are held in place on vise jaws by way of their magnetic back.

Sun Belt Products

Magnetic Soft Jaw Vise Pads are patented vise accessories that are made of tough, flexible polyvinyl chloride (PVC) and flexible magnetic strips. The pads come in a standard 5in length, although special orders for different lengths can be made to accommodate any vise. Wrapping delicate auto parts in rags or cloths to protect their finish while they are secured in a vise will not always prevent scratches. These inexpensive Vise Pads do a much better job of securing those kinds of parts, and, since their texture is soft, parts have little chance of being damaged. They are perfect for gently but firmly holding brass fittings, electronic components, gears, axles, shafts, cams, hydraulic parts, and numerous other highly polished items.

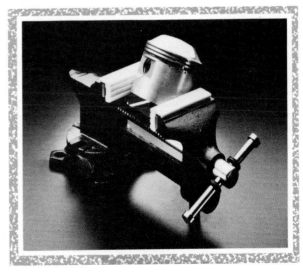

Burke Equipment Corporation

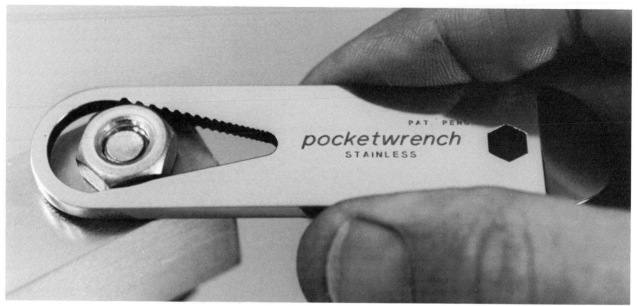

One ideal and handy tool to carry in your car or truck toolbox is the Pocketwrench. It will grip fasteners in both American sizes from 3/16in to 11/16in and metric sizes from 5mm to 17mm, square or hex. A self-tightening gripping action allows the Pocketwrench to grasp onto many fasteners that standard wrenches cannot. The tool also features a variable-width straight-blade screwdriver that doubles as a mini–pry bar for opening paint and other similar cans. The 1/4in hex socket can be placed over hex-drive bits for use as a handle. This tool weighs only 2 ounces. It is 4in long and 1in wide. Made of 400-series high-carbon stainless steel, it is polished to a mirrorlike finish, has a torque rating of 300lb-in, and has a lifetime guarantee.

CooperTools

The *CooperTools Catalog* is filled with familiar name brand tools and equipment, like those from Crescent, Lufkin, Weller, and more. In addition, CooperTools offers three other catalogs: *Industrial Tools, Electronics* and *Chains, Fittings, Blocks, and Lifting Clamps.* CooperTools provides quality tools and equipment for professional, industrial, and do-it-yourself craftspeople.

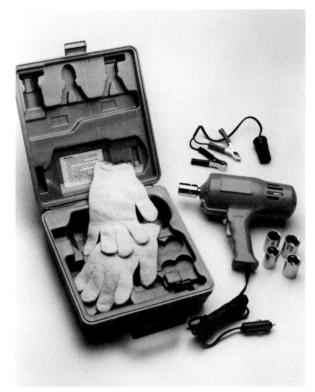

The Turner SI-90 Self-Igniting Refillable Torch from Cooper-Tools requires no matches or spark lighters for ignition. Just turn on the valve and press the ignitor switch for instant-on capability. The Turner SI-90 portable torch is designed to burn up to 30 minutes between refills. It can be used with propane or high-temperature fuel. This versatile torch may be used alone in tight, hard-to-reach areas or attached to a small cylinder for jobs that require extended burn times. With an adapter hose, it can be attached to a bulk tank with easy-disconnect. The torch features a comfortable, nonslip, fire retardant handle that can be used by either hand. It also comes with a stand for use on stationary work.

Flat tires are a problem everyone will have to contend with eventually at some point; they are an inevitable dilemma. For many, adjusting car jacks and removing wheel covers can be accomplished with ease. Removing lug nuts, on the other hand, can pose perplexing problems, especially if they have been torqued exceptionally tight. To make the removal of lug nuts an easy task, consider the Touch-Torque. The Touch-Torque tire wrench is a reversible lug wrench that operates on 12volts DC and was designed to replace all types of manual lug wrenches for the removal and proper replacement of flat tires. This tool generates 130lb-ft of torque, making it strong enough to remove quickly and safely the tightest lug nuts installed by a factory or repair shop. Lug nuts are also put back in place with this same torque power. The Touch-Torque tire wrench is stored in its own carrying case with handle and includes both metric and standard sockets, a 15ft power supply cord, a convenient lighter plug or battery clip adapter, and a pair of work gloves.

OMNIVERSE Research

Intermark World Products

Auto enthusiasts who spend a lot of time in off-road and racing activities should take a look at the MIGMASTER Portable Welder. All one needs to complete a MIG welding chore while a long way from a source of electricity is the MIGMASTER, a cordless 3/8in variable-speed drill, and two 12volt DC auto batteries connected in series. Drill speed is used to control the wire speed, which controls the welding amperage. MIGMASTER comes equipped with a shielding gas valve ready to handle your choice of shielding gases. By using any one of the available 4in spools of self-shielding steel wire, however, no gas is required for welding steel. To weld aluminum or stainless steel, simply change to the appropriate wire, connect the correct shielding gas for the wire chosen, and flip on the shielding gas valve. In the shop, MIGMASTER can also be used as a spool gun with most 220 to 440volt stick welders simply by connecting the unit to the hot lead. With a wide range of from 30amps to 200amps plus, MIGMASTER has the ability to weld 26-gauge to 1/2in-thick steel or 2/25in and thicker aluminum. As an option, you can purchase a complete MIGMASTER kit, which includes two 12volt batteries, a cordless 3/8in variable-speed drill and charging unit, instructions, and all cables. Cables are easily set up for charging both batteries at the same time. This tool welds as well as any welder of its capacity, including joining thin metal to thick metal and aluminum.

The vast majority of auto repair and maintenance efforts are conducted during daylight or under the bright lights of a workshop or garage at night. What happens, however, when your car or truck breaks down at night? Flashlights work fine when trying to illuminate a specific item, like a lug nut or distributor cap, but wouldn't a superbright light be a great asset when trying to set points or trace a shorted wire? The RC-500K Cordless Rechargeable Spotlight is just such a tool for those dark auto repair situations. With 500,000 candle-power, this is the most powerful rechargeable cordless portable light available. A computer-designed parabolic reflector casts the light's beam up to a mile. The unit will recharge from a 110volt AC home outlet or any 12volt car or vehicle outlet, like a lighter.

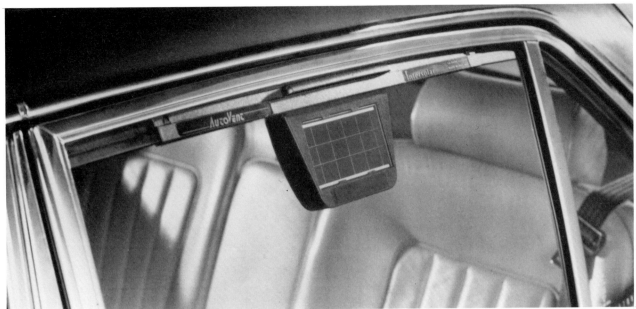

Hot summer days are uncomfortable, and they are made much worse when you have to hop into an automobile that has baked in the sun for hours with the windows rolled up. This situation is not good for the vehicle's interior, either. AutoVent was developed to eliminate problems of heat build-up inside cars while at the same time allowing for vehicles' security with rolled-up windows and locked doors.

AutoVent fits on the rear window of most cars; is maintenance free, weatherproof, and impact resistant; and will not drain any car's battery, as it is solar powered. Bright daylight and sunshine activate the AutoVent's fan as the solar panel converts light into electricity. The fan extracts heat, odors, and stale air and also draws fresh air into the vehicle's interior. AutoVent changes the air in the car every 15 minutes.

Maresh Industries

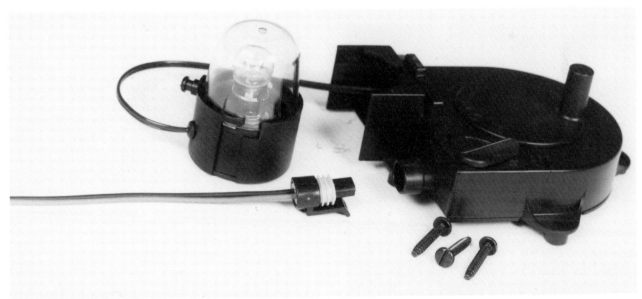

The Reel Light is a 12volt emergency light designed to be mounted on vehicles and then connected to the electrical system by way of a moisture-tight plug. The actual light module is removable and features an 18ft cord. When you are finished with the light, its cord reels back into the mounting base and the light locks into position securely so that it won't fall out. The unit has a built-in on-off switch and

a scratch resistant magnetic base, which allows the light module to hang onto any steel surface. The 12volt light bulb is replaceable, and the unit is resistant to dust, moisture, vibration, shocks, and corrosion. Each Reel Light comes with a mounting base, a moisture-tight electrical plug, and three 1in sheet metal mounting screws.

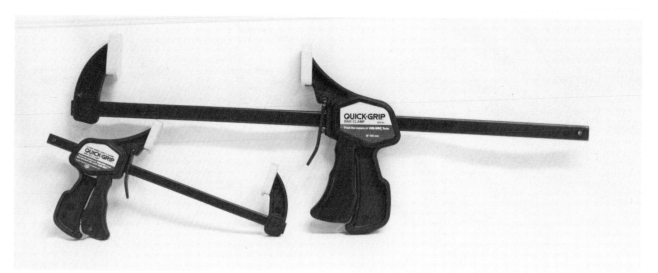

QUICK-GRIP Clamps are handy, versatile, easy-to-use, and strong. They are designed for one-handed operation to allow automotive repair people to clamp components together with one hand while positioning work and performing other related tasks with their other hand. A release lever lets the hardened steel bar slide freely through the grip and handle. QUICK-GRIP's pistol grip tightens the bar in $1/4$in increments and locks it to the work. Jaw pressure is applied evenly and does not incorporate conventional rotation torque, so items will not twist out of position under pressure. The clamps are equipped with soft protective pads that are removable and will not mar surfaces, meaning they are perfect for fiberglass operations. These tools work well for holding interior panels in place while screws are tightened, securing body panels while they are attached, and holding mechanical parts in position while related repairs or adjustments are made near them. QUICK-GRIP Clamps are also useful for pulling parts into place for connection, pressing suspension bushings together, and lining up ball joint control arms. When repairing or replacing disc brakes, these clamps compress and hold brake caliper pistons. QUICK-GRIP Clamps are available in five sizes ranging from 6in to 36in long, including a model that features a corner bracket and pad.

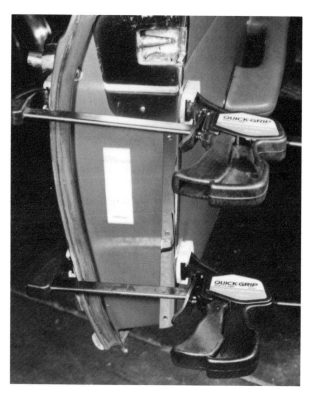

Helsper Sewing Company

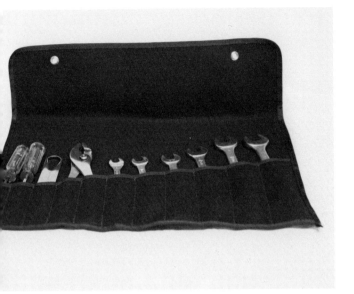

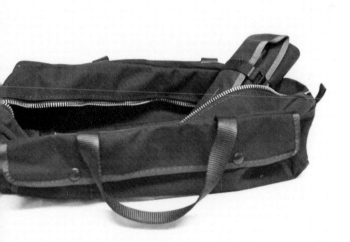

For convenient, rattle- and rust-free tool storage under a seat or in the trunk of your vehicle, consider heavy-duty canvas products like the Roll-Up Tool Pouch from Sewn Products. It measures 18in by 18in in the flat position and features a heavy-duty web strap and buckle closure. Two brass grommets at the top corners are used for hanging the pouch on a wall. The Roll-Up Pouch is designed to carry a full set of combination wrenches or an assortment of hand tools. The Mechanics Tool Bag is a heavy-duty product constructed of tough cotton duck canvas that has been treated to be water-repellant and mildew resistant. Both sides have compartment pockets with flaps. Hardboard bottoms are completely sewn into each bag and are not exposed. Heavy-duty nylon thread stitching and a large, solid brass zipper complement the bag's ruggedness. Tool Bags are available in two sizes: 6in by 6in by 12in and 6in by 6in by 18in.

Plano Molding Company

Looking through cans of nuts, bolts, washers, and other small items has been made a great deal easier with the Model #505 Sorta-Neat Organizer. This will replace those coffee cans, junk drawers, and breakable glass jars strewn about your workshop or garage. Cans of loose fasteners and other items are dumped out on the tray to make it easy for you to find what you're looking for. When finished, just snap the empty storage cup onto the end of the tray, then lift the tray to pour items back into their cup. The tray is hinged, and units come with five storage cups. The organizer measures 20¹/₂in long by 4³/₄in wide by 6³/₄in high.

The Plano Molding Company manufactures a wide range of toolboxes and handy organizers of all kinds. The three-drawer Model #873 Professional Toolbox (top center in photo) has a deep top for large tools and recessed top and side handles for easy carrying. A lock bar, along with solid brass hardware, keeps the box secure. The unit weighs 11lb and measures 21¹/₄in long, 12¹/₂in wide, and 12³/₄in high. The Power Tool Box at left features a handy tool tray that has storage underneath and measures 6⁷/₁₆in deep. This might be just the right unit for carrying a couple of power tools along with their accessories. Individual Plano toolboxes and storage units can be set up to carry just a specific assortment of tools and equipment geared for separate automotive repair, maintenance, or customizing operations. One box could contain all the supplies necessary for pinstripe and lettering jobs, another could hold sanders and sandpaper sheets for paint preparation, and so on.

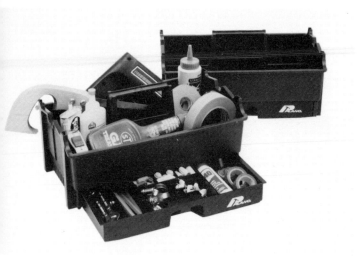

The Model #311R Tote-More Toolbox is equipped with a drawer for additional storage. It can be loaded up with a lot of the tools and small parts needed for various maintenance and repair jobs that commonly require assortments of connectors and fasteners, like sound system installations and upholstery repair. This box is made from 100 percent recycled plastic.

Almost every do-it-yourself auto enthusiast has a difficult time throwing away any usable screw, nut, bolt, washer, clip, or connector, or anything that may come in handy some day. An ideal container for all of those loose things is the Model #501 Storage Box. It has an opening at the top that is convenient for dropping things into, and the clear front face allows you to see what's inside. In addition, the front face opens up for sorting through items and can be closed without spilling contents. For more meticulous storage, consider the Model #974 Sortaway Organizer. It consists of four large boxes that can be divided into any number or configuration of compartments with the use of separate plastic partitions. This organizer can be mounted to a wall, or a number of them can be stacked one on top of another.

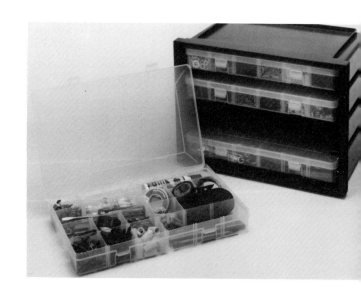

The Model #574 Sorta-Neat Tote is a tool and part holder. The open top can hold the tools used most often, and a recessed back compartment can hold big tools. Four tilt-out front compartments have a total of sixteen storage bins for different fasteners and other small items. The front compartments open automatically with a push-latch mechanism. A drill bit selector holder and an inch-to-millimeter ruler are built in. This unit measures 19½in high by 13½in wide by 8¼in deep.

Snap-on Tools Corporation

With the KR1010 End Cab, owners of the Snap-on KR1000B Roll Cab Tool Chest can add seven big drawers of storage. KR storage units feature double-wall construction and beams and stiffeners that are strategically placed to create strong, durable units. Drawers are made from 20-gauge steel and designed with ball bearing slides for quiet, easy operation. Precut drawer liners are provided to help protect drawer bottoms; a rubber top mat is also included. Another optional accessory for Snap-on tool chests is the KRA311 Storage Riser. It is designed to fit between the Roll Cab and top chest. The Riser bolts onto the cab and can be adjusted to three height settings: 3in, 7in, and 11in. The Riser offers a perfect place for storing manuals, personal items, and other things so that they are out of the way and do not block the top chest's drawers. It can also make for a handy worktable area. With more load capacity than a 1ton pickup truck, the big KR1000B Roll Cab provides an enormous 34,158ci of storage capacity. This unit also offers a big working surface measuring 29in by 52^{13}/$_{16}$in, and comes with a standard full vinyl protective mat.

Many window cranks and door handles are held onto shafts by special C-shaped wire clips. Fooling around with a long, skinny screwdriver to remove them could easily result in tears on door panels. The Trim Tool was made just for removing C-shaped wire clips. This tool comes as part of the Trim Removal Set, which also includes a special tool used for removing windshield molding clips and another for lifting off interior door panels.

Snap-on's BC5500 Super Charger 100/70amp battery charger is designed for use on both 6volt and 12volt automotive batteries and is capable of continuous charge, timed charge, and cranking assist. It can be adjusted for specific battery types but should only be used on 6volt and 12volt lead-and-acid batteries. The unit is portable and moves easily on 7in semi-pneumatic rubber tires. The Super Charger has three controls: two for charge rate (coarse and fine) and one for length of charge.

The Soft Lifter Jack Pad, shown here on the jack, will protect the detailed undercarriage of special cars that must be raised with a hydraulic floor jack. This pad measures 5in by 5in and will fit on any 2-, 2¼-, or 2½-ton hydraulic floor jack. Just like the standard cradles featured on floor jacks, the Soft Lifter is equipped with a 1⅛in center post. This item is ideal for use on vehicles with smartly painted or chromed under-carriage parts.

While working under any vehicle, keeping track of tools, nuts, bolts, and washers can be a difficult chore. Sockets can roll down driveways, nuts and washers might be misplaced under tires, and other items may lie hidden under creepers. The Tool Creeper features a handy permanent magnetic strip that keeps small parts from disappearing, lift handles for easy carrying to jobs, four fully rotating ball bearing casters for easy moving, and a rugged industrial-grade paint job on a heavy-gauge 11in square steel platform.

Case is using the Deluxe-Pro Bend-A-Light to improve his visibility while working in the engine compartment of his 1981 Ferrari 308 GTSi. This tool is perhaps the most useful item anyone could ask for when trying to find a washer or nut that has been accidentally knocked over into a dark engine crevice. The Bend-A-Light's flexible high-intensity light is made of a brass alloy. It will bend to any shape and illuminate hard-to-reach areas where conventional lighting could not possibly fit. Its $1/8$in-diameter bulb creates a brilliant light beam that penetrates almost anywhere. It has a 10in flexible shaft, is 26in in overall length, and features a magnetic clip-on base so that it can be temporarily mounted on a fender apron or other metal part. It also has a standard magnet pickup tip. Quite simply, a plastic tube is outfitted with a cylindrical magnet at one end. The open end of the tube slips over the light bulb. With the light lit to illuminate a space, this magnetic tip can be accurately maneuvered over a washer, nut, or bolt for easy pickup.

Those who work on cars know how valuable a pry bar can be when working with heavy parts that must be moved. Sometimes, a crowbar can fit where needed and complete a prying job with little problem. Other times, though, you may need the slim design of the tools in the Pry Bar Set, with screwdriverlike tips, to fit into tight spots and pry parts loose.

They can also be used as levers to help place heavy parts accurately. Whenever working with pry bars, you must recognize that metal items can chip. To reduce greatly the possibility of eye or face injury from flying metal chips or splinters, plan to wear a full face shield.

Spark Plug Plugs are designed to fit into and seal off spark plug holes while work is being done to the block. These plugs are used when detailing engines to take the place of spark plugs while painting the block. They can also be used when rebuilding engines to seal off cylinders during sandblasting or other dusty work. In addition, they do a good job of protecting the threads in spark plug holes.

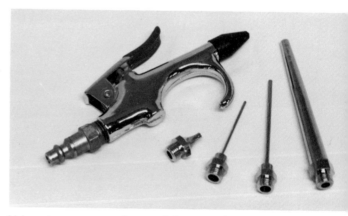

Using air pressure to clean and dry parts during repairs or detailing endeavors is made easier and more accurate with the 5-Piece Blow Gun Set. Along with the air gun and its rubber tip are four nozzles ranging from $1/16$in to $1/8$in in diameter and 2in to 4in in length. Each piece is chrome-plated for long life and resistance to a variety of auto workshop materials. The small nozzle tips offer users pinpoint accuracy when blowing out intricate electrical, automatic transmission, and other component parts. The air inlet connection nipple shown here does not come with the set. You must provide this part to make sure it is compatible with the air hose couplings featured on your air compressor system.

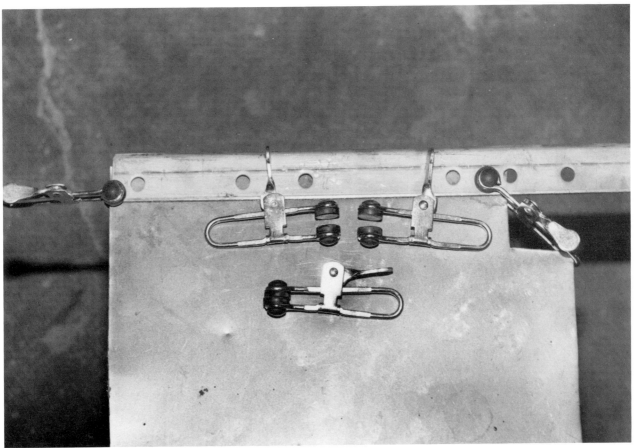

Quick Lock Clamps are sturdy, chrome-plated, rubber-padded products that will help you during all kinds of repair and restoration endeavors. They may not be big in size, but they have a grip that is second to none. The rubber pads protect surfaces against scratches, making these items ideal for installing door skins and working with polished panels. They come in packages of ten and can be used to hold pieces together when welding, gluing, riveting, and so on. Their positive-grip locking system leaves no room for error; once locked, they stay locked.

The Baldor Buffer/Grinder is a 1/3hp, 3600rpm, 6in combination buffer-grinder built for rugged use. The standard wire brush wheel makes quick work of removing rust, scale, and debris from neglected exhaust clamps and myriad other metal parts. Large clear shields provide plenty of work visibility and are easily adjustable for any size job. Tool rests are also widely adjustable in horizontal, vertical, and angled positions. This machine is quiet and smooth and offers a great deal of torque. While grinding or cleaning small auto parts, consider using a pair of VISE-GRIPs or other locking tools to keep parts firmly secure. Optional accessories for this buffer-grinder include items such as the Scotchbrite Cleaning and Polishing Wheels, Buffing Wheels, Wheel Dresser, and more.

Pine Ridge Enterprise

Automobile restoring, building, customizing, and concours detailing require a great deal of time, money, patience, and work. The effort put forth to make cars and trucks beautiful is admirable and appreciated. Unfortunately, no amount of attention can enable these pristine vehicles to look perfect forever. Moisture in the atmosphere, air pollution, and a host of other elements seem to be constantly working against meticulous restoration and detailing efforts to cause automobiles eventually to go downhill. Serious restorers and dedicated concours d'elegance competitors sometimes build separate structures solely for storing their vehicles. These buildings are equipped with humidity and temperature controls, sealed off from *unfiltered* outside and possibly polluted air, and secured like a downtown bank vault. This is great for those who can afford such extravagance, but what can the so-called regular car owner do? The answer lies in the OMNIBAG, a giant plastic "sandwich bag" designed to keep air, moisture, and other unwanted things away from precious vehicles in storage. Vehicles sealed in the bag correctly have emerged months later in exactly the same condition they were in on the day they were wrapped up. No dust, no rust, no moisture condensation, and no upholstery deterioration. Sealed plastic bags work great for food storage, so why not for auto storage? The OMNIBAG is designed for just one season of protection, but conscientious and meticulous users may find they can use it more than once. Small tears or rips can be resealed with heavy-duty duct tape, and desiccant packs can be thoroughly dried in a regular or microwave oven. After making sure that windows have been rolled *down,* Case wraps the antenna on his 1968 Jaguar E Type roadster with cardboard and duct tape to prevent it from puncturing the OMNIBAG. Rolled up much like a sock, the OMNIBAG is gently pulled over the front of the car. It takes at least two people to properly insert a car into the OMNIBAG, and four sets of hands make it an easy task. For those deeply concerned about extralight scratches on paint, consider first covering the car with a *breathable* cotton car cover. After desiccants, cardboard drip pans, and mothballs have been placed inside the OMNIBAG, Wentworth uses a regular household vacuum cleaner to suck out the air from inside the OMNIBAG protecting his sport truck. This will cause something of a vacuum seal around his truck and remove a lot of the moisture that was present in the air that was drawn out. Heavy-duty clamps provided with the OMNIBAG pinch off excess bag and essentially seal the vehicle inside an airtight, dust- and moisture-free bag. The results of 5 minutes of vacuum cleaner time are obvious, as the OMNIBAG clings to Wentworth's sport truck.

Sources

The following companies provided information, photos, and samples of their automotive tool products. Much of the information provided by these companies about their products was paraphrased and sometimes quoted from product descriptions. To learn more about the tools and equipment featured in this book, as well as to obtain catalogs and information about the great many additional products carried by these companies, you are encouraged to call or write the firms themselves.

Aeroquip Corporation
Industrial Connectors Group
3000 Strayer
Maumee, OH 43537
419-238-1190

Alden Corporation
Munson Road
P.O. Box 6262
Wolcott, CT 06716
800-832-5336

American Tool Companies
P.O. Box 337
De Witt, NE 68341
402-683-2315

Autotronic Controls Corporation
MSD Ignition
1490 Henry Brennan Drive
El Paso, TX 79936
915-855-7123

Black and Decker
Automotive Products Group
10 North Park Drive
P.O. Box 798
Hunt Valley, MD 21030-0748
800-762-6672

Bug Brick Products
1633 West Lake Road, #7
Belle Glade, FL 33430
407-996-3634

Burke Equipment Corporation
P.O. Box 28264

Kansas City, MO 64118
800-467-6378

California Car Cover Company
15430 Cabrito Road
Van Nuys, CA 91406
800-423-5525

The Chamberlain Group
845 Larch Avenue
Elmhurst, IL 60126
800-528-9131

Chief Automotive Systems
P.O. Box 1368
Grand Island, NE 68802-1368
800-445-9262

CooperTools
P.O. Box 728
Apex, NC 27502
919-362-7510

Dremel
4915 Twenty-first Street
Racine, WI 53406-9989
414-554-1390

Eagle Equipment Company
23 Wetherell Place
Plainville, MA 02762
800-535-0016

The Eastwood Company
580 Lancaster Avenue, Box 296
Malvern, PA 19355
800-345-1178

Empire Brushes
P.O. Box 1606
U.S. 13 North
Greenville, NC 27835
919-758-4111

Foreign Car Specialties
101 South Avenue
Tallmadge, OH 44278
216-633-3302

Haack Products
14177 Nola
Livonia, MI 48154
313-459-4144

Harbor Freight Tools
3491 Mission Oaks Boulevard
Camarillo, CA 93011
800-423-2567

Helsper Sewing Company
Sewn Products
36 Center Drive, Unit 3
Gilberts, IL 60136
708-428-5462

Hemmings Motor News
P.O. Box 100
Bennington, VT 05201
800-227-4373

HTP America
261 Woodwork Lane, Department ATBG
Palatine, IL 60067
800-872-9353

Intermark World Products
632 Green Bay Road
Kenilworth, IL 60043
708-256-6500

Jacobs Electronics
500 North Baird Street
Midland, TX 79701
800-626-8800

Jericho Products
2444 Moorpark Avenue, Suite 300
San Jose, CA 95128
408-978-3873

Kent-Moore
SPX Corporation
28635 Mound Road
Warren, MI 48092
800-345-2233

K. O. Lee Company
200 South Harrison
P.O. Box 1416
Aberdeen, SD 57402-1416
605-225-5820

Lions Automotive
P.O. Box 229
Lyons, IL 60538
708-484-2229

Lockdown Securities, Inc.
605 S. Adams Street
Laramie, WY 82070
307-745-5999

Makita U.S.A.
14930 Northam Street
La Mirada, CA 90638-5753
714-522-8088

Maresh Industries
10931 Ivy Lane
Orange, CA 92669
714-639-7987

Neward Enterprises
P.O. Box 725
Rancho Cucamonga, CA 91729-0725
800-648-9822

NTY International Corporation
111 Corporate Boulevard
South Plainfield, NJ 07080
800-342-5689

O.C.S. Shark File Sharpening System
371 Second Street
Chuluota, FL 32766
407-365-8860

OMNIVERSE Research
P.O. Box 33243
Los Gatos, CA 95031
408-354-6611

Parking Solutions
2663 Manhattan Beach Boulevard
Redondo Beach, CA 90278
800-359-5021

P.C.S.
2884 Trades West Road
Santa Fe, NM 87501
505-471-6200

Pine Ridge Enterprise
13165 Center Road
Bath, MI 48808
517-641-4881

Plano Molding Company
431 East South Street
Plano, IL 60545-0189
708-552-3111

Porter-Cable Corporation
4825 Highway 45 North
P.O. Box 2468
Jackson, TN 38302-2468
901-668-8600

Pro Motorcar Products
22025 U.S. Highway 19 North
Clearwater, FL 34625
800-323-1090

Right Angle Tool Company
200 South Normal
Macomb, IL 61455
800-828-2043

Sears Roebuck and Company
P.O. Box 239
Bellwood, IL 60104
800-366-3000

SEFIDCo Tool Products Group
P.O. Box 3305
La Jolla, CA 92038
619-944-9900

Sidewinder Products Corporation
320 Second Avenue North
Birmingham, AL 35204
800-999-3405

Smithy Company
3023 East Second Street
The Dalles, OR 97058
800-345-6342

Snap-on Tools Corporation
2801 Eightieth Street
Kenosha, WI 53141-1410
800-866-5748

Steelcrafters
440 Matson Road
Jonesborough, TN 37659
615-928-8962

Sun Belt Products
11215 North Fifty-second Avenue
Glendale, AZ 85304
602-678-1503

Sunchaser Tools
3202 East Foothill Boulevard
Pasadena, CA 91107
818-795-1588

TiP Sandblast Equipment
7075 Route 446
P.O. Box 649
Canfield, OH 44406
800-321-9260

Vermont American
P.O. Box 340
Lincolnton, NC 28093-0340
704-735-7464

WESCO Autobody Supply
12532 NE 124th Street
Kirkland, WA 98033
206-823-5887

William K. Westley Company
9545 Midwest Avenue, Suite D
Garfield Heights, OH 44125-2340
800-858-6605

Index